AMAZING i

From Global Recoruings Network

Editor, Allan Starling

75th Anniversary Edition

AMAZING STORIES

From Global Recordings Network (GRN)

Editor, Allan Starling

75th Anniversary Edition

Global Recordings Network
41823 Enterprise Circle N. Suite 200
Temecula, CA 92590

Tel. 951.719.1650

Cover and Interior Design: David Gutierrez

All accounts in this book are based on actual people and events. Some names of people, places or languages have been changed for security purposes.

Unless otherwise indicated, all Scripture quotations are taken from the Holy Bible, New Living Translation, copyright © 1996, 2004, 2007 by Tyndale House Foundation.

Used by permission of Tyndale House Publishers, Inc., Carol Stream, Illinois 60188. All rights reserved.

ISBN-13: 978-1494741709

ISBN-10: 1494741709

Contents

- Contents -

- Amazing Stories -

FORWARD
Everyone loves a story

Down through the centuries, storytelling has been an effective way to communicate. It was Jesus' most common form of teaching. Oral learners use it as their primary way of communicating and teaching. The motto of Global Recordings Network (GRN) is Telling the Story of Jesus in Every Language.

The process of telling that story has generated its own narratives. There are accounts about how GRN started, how we find the languages, and how we make the recordings. There are features about how we place the recordings into the hands of the people, how they listen to the recordings, and evidence of the unfinished task.

The amazing stories span 75 years of technology covering the use of phonograph records, audio cassettes, CDs, MP3s, websites, and smart phones. More are waiting to be told. Make yourself comfortable and enjoy reading this collection.

- Amazing Stories -

THE BEGINNING

Our opening tale is set on the occasion when Joy Ridderhof visited Stuart and Molly Mill in Sydney, Australia in 1952. She told them how she began the small ministry that later grew to become Global Recordings Network.

The rest of this book presents the kinds of accounts Joy loved to hear—and we are confident you will too. You can read of how countless people from thousands of language groups have come to faith in Christ through hearing the life-giving message of the Gospel on the recordings.

Joy Ridderhof

Over the years the technology has changed, but the results are the same, and the retelling is just as inspiring. It's our pleasure to share this collection with you.

- Amazing Stories -

How it All Began

Stuart Mill - Lost for Words

Around a cheery fireplace in Sydney, Australia, Joy Ridderhof told her story. A missionary to Honduras in Central America from 1931, she learned deep lessons of faith and dependence upon God. Returning to the United States in 1937, it seemed that dysentery and malaria had weakened her so much her missionary service was over.

Joy was the youngest of a large family. None of them dreamt that little Joy could do anything of

1930s wind-up gramophone

great significance. But while she was recuperating at home, and unable to return to the Hondurans she had come to love, she reflected that perhaps gramophone records could be the means of reaching them with the Gospel in their own language.

Flat on her back in her father's house in Los Angeles, California, she prayed for guidance. Her friends neglected her; her church forgot her; she was just a burnt-out missionary. She had no idea of the complexities of the world's languages. She would have been overwhelmed to learn that there were over 7,000 major languages worldwide and thousands more dialects. But in her small room, her faith burned brightly.

"I remembered the raucous sound of gramophone records being played in the saloons and shops of Honduras," she recalled, "and how I had been playing hymns in English on the gramophone when a fellow missionary observed wistfully, 'If we only had Gospel recordings in Spanish.'"

Joy's eyes searched the ceiling as her mind went back to her childhood days. Her stern Dutch-born father, Professor

Ridderhof, had unexpectedly brought home a second-hand cylindrical gramophone. She smiled to herself at the memory of his horror as he discovered that some of the recordings were comic songs and dance tunes, whereupon he promptly destroyed them.

"As I lay on my sick bed, I could still remember them, nearly a quarter of a century later," she said. "The constant, unchanging repetition had imprinted itself on my mind so much it couldn't be removed."

Joy followed her train of thought to a logical conclusion: Why couldn't she harness this imprinting for the Gospel?

"I thought of gramophone records that kept on saying the same thing over and over again, without getting tired," she said enthusiastically. "I began to think how wonderful it would be if someone could produce Spanish records to sing and preach the Gospel."

After her health improved, Joy Ridderhof began to see what God could do to make her dream come true. Providentially, she had made an acquaintance when in Central America who had some professional equipment in his home in Los Angeles.

"When I called on him," she said, eyes alight, "I found he was not only willing to cooperate with me, but to work on a non-profit basis."

"On the last day of 1938, I went to the studio, to make my first Gospel recording in Spanish. To soundproof, the room, he had draped it with blankets and quilts. There was no audience, just a technician. We taped hymns and verses of Scripture in Spanish, words that were to be reproduced hundreds of times, to be listened to over and over again in remote little towns and hamlets in Honduras."

The cost of that historic session was just $15.00.

About half a dozen copies of this first recording were produced in 1939 and sent to the missionary who had taken Joy's place on the field with the request that they be put into the hands of the people to take into their homes. Back came an enthusiastic letter.

"Please send me more. The people are listening, and understanding the message. Some have already accepted the Lord and been converted."

Joy's eyes were moist as she added, "This turned out to be God's answer to my prayer for some means of spreading the Gospel and the Word of God rapidly throughout the scattered villages of Honduras."

Later, she rejoiced to recall that some 200 recordings of that initial script had been made in Spanish and had gone to other Spanish-speaking areas.

In no time at all, a new fledgling agency called Spanish Gospel Recordings was begun. Its beginnings were humble. Joy's attic bedroom in Los Angeles was also her office. For a time she stood alone, with no one to support her, no board or advisory council.

News of the recordings spread quickly, and missionaries from other countries who spoke other languages began requesting recordings in their own peoples' heart languages. "I come from Tanzania and speak Swahili," wrote one. Another challenged her, "What about India? I can speak Urdu. Please, will you make us some recordings?"

Joy hesitated, shrewdly suspecting that many men would be disinclined to back a venture of this nature. Instead, she turned in faith to the Lord.

Lord, what do you want me to do? You know there are millions of Spanish-speaking people in the world. That's more than enough for any one person to serve. But how, Lord, are people of every kindred and tongue and nation going to hear as you say in your word?

That they should hear was her constant prayer. Worldwide demand for her Gospel recordings increased so much that finally Joy prayed, Lord I'll make them in any language you want, but on one understanding. You will have to pay all the bills. With that in mind, she dropped the word 'Spanish' from the title and it became simply Gospel Recordings.

Joy never had cause to regret the bargain she made with God that day. Seventy-five years later, the mission thrives on that same dependence upon an all-providing God.

Tape recorder technology was in its infancy in the early days of the mission and bulky machines littered the floor of the renovated stable in the back yard of the Ridderhof home on Witmer Street.

A small team of volunteers helped Joy and her friends move the accumulated junk. All worked together on the same basis; there was no pay-day and God had to meet all their needs.

Joy could clearly envisage what she needed in order to record in primitive tribal situations, but after World War II, very little was immediately available. Portability was crucial, but at that stage miniaturization of equipment was virtually unknown. Besides, recording tape in those days was made of paper, was fragile, and apt to break without warning.

Ex-submariner Herman Dyk came as an answer to prayer. Trained in electronics, he and engineer Al Rethey, put together what has been claimed to be the first-ever portable tape recorder. A later, vastly improved version was extremely suitable. Joy was delighted and in faith asked them to build twelve more. By today's standards these players were enormous. Joy and her companions had been shown how to service them, but as her co-worker Sanna Barlow remarked, with a twinkle in her eye, "When we've done our best, and they still sometimes won't work, we slap them and start rejoicing. Somehow the Lord gets them going."

Milestones
What's in a Name?

Allan Starling

A change of name often signifies an important milestone in the life of a person or organization. Our mission has had several name changes over the last 75 years, and each of them has been linked to a significant change.

The Original Vision

When Joy Ridderhof first conceived the idea of using records to reach oral communicators in Honduras, she named her fledgling organization Spanish Gospel Recordings. Putting her vision into practice with no funding or technical expertise demanded a huge step of faith. She faced enormous hurdles like finding speakers and singers, making the recordings, paying for manufacturing the records and getting them into the hands of the Spanish speaking people in Honduras. It wasn't long before the recordings were finding their way all over Latin America. But even so the vision was limited to one language – Spanish. And this was reflected in the name.

Then one day someone came to Joy with a request that would usher in a colossal change in focus.

The Second Language – Navajo

In her book, Faith by Hearing, Phyllis Thompson tells about some missionaries who asked Joy if she could make recordings in the Navajo language. Phyllis writes: "The request seemed simple enough. The missionaries were even prepared to travel to Los Angeles, bringing a Navajo with them. Why did she hesitate?

If records for Navajo, why not records for other peoples as well? Where would it end?" Look back, Larry Allmon, who succeeded Joy as Executive Director, wrote, "Joy Ridderhof's decision to record the second language (Navajo) in 1941 was a landmark in the history of world evangelization. This change in focus enabled [GRN] to extend the Good News to peoples speaking 5,000 languages! [GRN has] played no small part in the Lord's still-to-be-fulfilled promise that 'this Gospel shall be proclaimed ... to all peoples.'"

And so the name of the organization was shortened to Gospel Recordings. When the mission was incorporated in August, 1943, the name changed again to Gospel Recordings, Inc.

Going International

As the mission grew, branches were opened in various countries, with Los Angeles as headquarters. In February 1993, delegates from around the world met in London to form a new umbrella organization with twenty interdependent member countries, each with its own local board and staff, making it a truly international organization. And the new relationship found expression in a new name: Global Recordings Network.

Changing a name, especially one that has become well known in some circles, is not to be done lightly. But there were several good reasons for this change. The name Gospel Recordings became confused by some people in the USA as referring to the gospel music industry. On the other hand, some countries that were opposed to the spreading of the Christian Gospel saw it in a different light. The words 'Global' and 'Network' signified not only that the work had reached into all countries but that it had now decentralized into a network of over twenty interdependent organizations under one umbrella.

Of all the names we can think of, the most important are those of people from every language, tribe and nation that will be inscribed in the Lamb's Book of Life. Many of them will be there because they listened to a recording in their own language.

GETTING TO THE LANGUAGES

Over the last 75 years GRN has made numerous recordings in over six thousand languages. The first Spanish recordings were done in a make-shift studio in a home in Los Angeles. Very few recording artists came to our downtown office building. Instead, GRN field workers traveled to where the people lived, persuaded them to help, and made the recordings in their backyards.

Most of the language helpers would not call themselves recording artists. They are simply people who speak a language in which the message of salvation needs to be told. More often than not, they live in small villages, off the beaten track. Just getting to them is a story itself.

Finding the Wakindiga

Sanna Barlow - Light is Sown

TANZANIA, EAST AFRICA - The Wakindiga Language

It was at Kijota, in Tanzania, East Africa, where we first heard of the Wakindiga and began to make plans to catch their language. Nobody had mentioned these fast diminishing pygmy-type Bushmen as Joy, Ann, and I poured over the language maps and outlined our recording itinerary. At the time, our minds were occupied with other hard-to-get languages. Besides, neither the name for the people, Wakindiga, nor the language, Kindiga, showed on our maps.

In a casual conversation, we were unexpectedly introduced to the forest people who were often employed to assist hunters.

"They are small people, semi-pygmies," our missionary host, Howard Olson, told us. "But they can handle a taut bow seven feet high—their arrows go straight to the mark—never a miss."

From the moment we heard those words, we were tracking down the Wakindiga.

"What about the language of these guides?" we asked. "It must be distinctly different."

"Different? Is it ever," he exclaimed. "Full of all kinds of weird clicks. No other African can understand them."

"Do you suppose we could get one of these people for making records?" Joy wondered.

Howard shook his head. "Now you're asking for a miracle sure enough. But it would be something to have records for these people. As it is, they are impossible to reach because they understand scarcely any Swahili, and of course no one else can speak their language. They are a dying-out tribe you know—very few of them now—between five hundred and two thousand. Nobody knows exactly."

As he added bits and pieces of information, we became convinced that we needed to find them. Joy expressed it with no waver or thought of previous schedules and dates.

"We must get this language, by all means. We may have to take a long trip to find them. But we must. Small isolated peoples like this can be missed entirely unless they have the Gospel presented to them in their very own language." She stood up and paced the floor. "No group can be too small, for our concern is to reach the few, even the one—even the women, who do not figure in statistics on literacy—who could not understand unless they hear the message in their own language. These bush people are a priority for records because none of the usual avenues of evangelism can reach them. We must get this language. We cannot leave these parts until we do."

"The Wakindiga," Mr. Olson spoke slowly, thoughtfully, "are in the Yaida Swamps—but where? That's the question. They roam about as unpredictably as the game."

Joy was not deterred. "Didn't you say the hunters hired them as guides? How do they go about this? Couldn't we hire them in the same way for this work?"

Howard brightened. "Aha. A clue! The hunters first contact an African chief in the Yaida Swamp vicinity; and then he sends his runners to search for them." He stopped, and thought for a moment. "But there's another problem. These Wakindiga know only a few phrases of Swahili, the trade language. How will you make them understand the material?"

Joy persisted, "Do these Wakindiga know the language of, say, the predominant tribe on their borders?"

"Ah yes. It's very likely some may know Isanzu pretty well."

"Then the task is not impossible," Joy beamed. We can communicate with them through our English, to the missionary's Swahili, to an African who knows both Swahili and Isanzu. He, in turn, can give the short simple sentence to the Wakindiga man who understands Isanzu, and can then speak the thought in his own language. Once a sentence is recorded, we play it and check it back again from the bush language to Isanzu, to Swahili, and to English. It can be done."

Now convinced the quest for Wakindiga records was a real possibility, Mr. Olson's next contribution was, "I know the man who can help you. He spent part of his vacation recently on a hunt in the Yaida Swamps, and he knows the right chief to approach. It is Dean Peterson at Isambi, and you plan to go there."

Days were filled with the making of records in many other important languages representing large tribes. But from then on, the search for Wakindiga became a special matter of prayer. At Isambi in Dean Peterson's office we studied his large map of the Yaida Swamp area, and noted Isanzu station—farther north and a little west of Isambi—was on its western border.

"I can send a runner today to Isanzu," said Dean eagerly, "and our request can be followed through by the missionary there, Bob Ward. He will see the chief."

Even before we left Isambi for our next assignment at Kinampanda, the runner was on his way to Isanzu. Our prayers kept pace with him. We detailed the request to God for a selection of the right helpers—those who could understand and who would work willingly and conscientiously.

Howard Olson had news for us. "The runner has returned from Isanzu, and Dean tells me the chief has given his word to fetch three Wakindiga to help you. He expects to have them there by Monday morning."

This was wonderful news, not only to us, but to the missionaries at Kinampanda who prayed with us that what at first seemed impossible would now become a reality.

You can listen to a recording of the Kindiga language at:
globalrecordings.net/en/language/1043

Completing the Picture

Allan Starling

Brad and Curt spent nine months as mission interns in a sensitive Asian country putting together a dialect puzzle. Scattered throughout the country, like jigsaw puzzle pieces, are groups of people who speak different languages and dialects. They are different sizes, shapes and colors, and they are often hard to identify.

How could the two men find those precious puzzle pieces? Like its jigsaw counterpart, the project required slow, methodical work, finding one dialect at a time, and fitting it into the overall picture. Fortunately they had help. With the aid of computers, maps, GPS devices, and information compiled by GRN and other missions, they were able to pinpoint the location of many dialects. With their interpreter they went on paths less traveled, met lots of people, and asked lots of questions. Because they were American students studying the culture, the government gladly assisted them. The information they gathered is now available to our field recordists and distributors who will take the puzzle a few more steps toward final completion.

The Bible tells us that one day the final puzzle will be complete and people from "every tribe and tongue and language" will sing praises around the throne (Rev 5:9).

What a beautiful picture that will be.

A Recordist's Diary

Valerie Deguchi

ZAIRE, CENTRAL AFRICA

Day 1. Arrive in Bukavu, Zaire, at 1:45 p.m. I can't believe it. Nothing has changed since my last visit five years ago. The customs officials are still unsalaried so their only income is what they can rip off from the tourists. Every time I come I hassle with them about all my recording equipment. They literally go through everything. I close up my suitcase. Now we talk.

Oh, oh. There's no one to meet me. It's a 50 km walk into town. Better find a ride quickly. H-E-L-P! Thank you Lord. The Mission Aviation Fellowship (MAF) people have not left yet, so maybe they will find room for me in their vehicle.

Day 2. Message – "Sorry, your flight has been cancelled until tomorrow." Lord, you know I can't afford to lose even one workday. Make the most of it. Get out your writing pad and answer those letters.

Day 3. I have to be ready by 5:30 a.m. It takes three hours to get to the airstrip and load the plane. Off we go, airborne at last. Oh, oh! I forgot to take my Dramamine pill. Out comes the black plastic bag. Lord, you never gave me the stomach for flying in these small planes!

From above, the great Ituri Forest looks like a soft green carpet. Lord, if we crash, there is no way we will find our way out. We arrive on a dirt airstrip. Perfect landing. Great pilot. Immediately we are swarmed by villagers.

The missionary interprets their questions. "Who is this stranger? What tribe is she from?"

Lord, this place must be close to hell. It's so hot and humid. I can feel my body burning up. It's like being in a giant sauna. Lord, I need a cold Coke. Sorry. No cokes, hamburgers or french-fries. But there is plenty of meat – snake, wild pig, chimpanzee and monkey. And when that's gone, there are giant bats. Lord please deaden my taste buds.

Day 4. I'm ready for recording. Let's get going, I only have two weeks here. The recordings are not going to go smoothly. I can feel it in my bones. It's preparation time. Meet with the missionaries. Pump them for information so that we can make the recordings more culturally relevant. Explain to the language helpers what takes place. Oh, no! It's going to rain hard. Lord, my quarters are made of mud walls with leaves for the roof. It's not going to leak is it? Midnight... plop, plop. Mud and rain. Where? Yep, right over my bed. What on earth is that thing crawling over my face — Wow. Three-inch cockroaches are all over! Hey, where's my shoe. SMASH. SQUISH. End of that one. Only 100 more to go.

Day 5. More research and more questions. Lord, please help us make these recordings communicate what You want.

Day 6. Someone in the village has died. Funerals are very much a part of African culture, so all work comes to a halt. I feel feverish. Lord, I can't afford to come down with malaria just now.

Day 7. Now down to serious recording work. By mid-afternoon the language helpers' heads begin to nod. It's hot and they aren't used to working full days. Come on folks, we can do a bit more. Out comes my bag of candies for energy.

Thank you Lord for a good day's work. My back is killing me

from sitting on these chairs. I need to walk. Everywhere I go kids follow me. Lord, I need some privacy. The only place is the 'choo' (toilet). Unfortunately, you can't sit. Only a hole. Lord, help me if one of these logs break! Don't laugh, it's happened before.

Day 8 and following. Lord, thank you. We are making progress. I can feel your presence and help. People are praying. The language helpers are tired, but when we speak on subjects like witchcraft, stealing, bribery, and adultery, I am encouraged to hear them say, "Hey, this is exactly what our people need to hear."

Lord how do we tell these people that they don't have to fear the spirits of the forest? These spirits do have power. Often deep chills go up my spine when we talk about the demon-possessed man in the Gospels. I'm recording on a very calm day. Suddenly the tree outside starts shaking. Is there a monkey up there? No, nothing visible to the human eye. "We wrestle not against flesh and blood but against ... the rulers of the darkness of this world" (Eph. 3:10).

Final day.

Lord, I've been sweaty and impatient. I've complained and longed for my departure. But I feel sad. I have come to appreciate these people and their daily struggles and fears. I'll miss them. Thank you, that I've been part of a team to bring them your message. Please help them to come to the Cross, and to know the joy and peace that only you can give. Help them to know that there is a greater power than their spirits.

Coincidences, Mistakes, or Warfare?

Told to Allan Starling

Names have been changed for security purposes

When we prepared to make recordings in a language related to Tibetan Buddhism, little did we know that it would take a year and a half to complete the project.

We prayed and planned for a long time. We could not go into Tibet, so we looked for someone in Nepal. Finally, we found a native speaker willing to speak on the recordings.

The man lived a long way from Kathmandu, Nepal. Just getting to him proved an adventure. Two of us planned to go by motorbike. The roads are treacherous, so we made sure the bike was in good working order. We carefully packed our recording equipment and started out. About fifteen kilometers down the road a tire went flat. There was no place to fix it. We had to pray and wait for help.

A truck driver stopped and offered help. We struggled to get the bike onto the back of the truck. Someone found a plank so we could roll it up. I had to sit in the back of the truck, balance myself, and hold the bike as we turned and weaved and bumped along. Later we were able to find some rope and tie the bike down.

We stopped at a small village only to discover that they could not help us. After gyrating for sixty kilometers we found a repair shop. The truck driver was patient, but we had to pay him a lot for his help. I wheeled the bike into the shop, only to find the mechanic wasn't there. Another man offered to help. He found a nail in the tire, replaced the tube, and sent us on our way.

I didn't go very far before I noticed that the bike was making a strange noise. It turned out the tire had not been replaced correctly and was rubbing against the frame.

Travel in Nepal is not easy, but we were having more than our fair share of problems. Was this caused just by chance or was there something more?

About ten kilometers down the road, the tire went flat again. We had to drag the bike two more kilometers to find a mechanic. He told us the new tube was no good. He didn't have a replacement, so patched it up as best he could. This time it took us forty kilometers before going flat. We finally found a new tube.

Much of the time allotted for the entire trip was spent just getting there. We arrived late and discovered that all the lodges were full, but our contact was able to find a place for us. The following day we began working with our language helper. We spent the morning explaining the process to him.

After lunch we were ready to begin but discovered that, despite our careful planning, we had left the scripts behind. We couldn't blame anyone but ourselves, even though it had never happened before. We had to wait until the following day to find a place where they could be faxed to us.

Finally we recorded the first sentence. But when I tried to play it back, nothing happened. Our Digital Audio Tape (DAT) machine had jammed. We couldn't open it, so we took it to several repair shops in the area. They were not successful either and explained that it needed a very small screwdriver. We wanted to give up, but we had travelled so far and with so much difficulty already. I was very frustrated and discouraged. I was certain now that the devil was doing everything he could to stop us from making those recordings. I prayed. Suddenly the Lord gave me the idea that a watchmaker should have a little screwdriver. Yes. He was able to open it. The tape was caught inside. This had never happened previously.

We went back to the language helper and he was very happy to get started again. But ten minutes into the recordings session – bang, bang – construction started in the next building. It had been abandoned for 6 months, but the very day we started recording, it was back in full swing. So we lost more time looking for another place to record. We prayed and asked the Lord to intervene in this spiritual warfare.

Despite all the setbacks we were able to make some good recordings before we returned to Kathmandu. With a sigh of relief, I transferred them from the DAT onto a laptop computer.

I used a special program to do the preliminary editing. This included removing many noises. I was busy editing when, without warning, the screen went blank. I lost all the data and had to reload it and re-edit. The next day the same thing happened.

People started to ask why the recordings weren't finished. I wanted to give them to those who could use them. But another delay occurred when I was forced to move my office.

It was two months before I was able to work on the editing again. I now had a new, faster, desktop computer with additional memory and was looking forward to using it.

I was ready to load the tape, but where was it? That DAT tape was very precious to me. It was the only message from the Bible in that language. I had made sure it was kept safe. I looked everywhere. I wanted to cry. I lifted my hand to the sky, Lord I surrender, I cannot do it. It is too much for me.

A picture of a backpack came to my mind. I found it and ran my hand over the side. I felt a DAT tape. But was it the tape? Yes. Thank you Lord.

The Bible tells us, "Our struggle is not against flesh and blood, but against the rulers, against the authorities, against the powers of this dark world and against the spiritual forces of evil in the heavenly realms" (Eph. 6:12).

Yes, making the recording involved many struggles, but as the scripture reminds us, "The Spirit who lives in you is greater than the spirit who lives in the world (1 John 4:4)."

On the Move

Valerie Deguchi

TANZANIA, EAST AFRICA

In order to make recordings in languages and dialects of Tanzania, my partner and I had to make our way to some remote areas. We soon discovered that travel is difficult in Tanzania if you don't have your own vehicle.

Our first destination was a small island in Lake Victoria. There was no gangplank, so to get on and off the three-deck ferry I had to jump. If I missed, it was about a 20-foot drop into yucky waters.

I made it!

Our contact didn't turn up – so my partner and I walked, walked and walked to another village. After two days, we finally found someone to speak on the recordings in the Kijita language.

It was very evident that the island was Satan's territory. A form of Folk Islam, which included witchcraft, was growing by leaps and bounds. But God gave a sense of peace. On more than one occasion I claimed God's promise that "greater is He that is in you, than He that is in the world (1 John 3:4)". I have never ceased to marvel at the power we have in the name of Jesus.

Our next trip was much longer. We missed the bus we had planned to take. Later we heard that it had overturned. One person was killed and many others were hurt. Thank you God for your protection!

The next bus left at 4:00 a.m. It was a relief to arrive at our destination after being bounced and tossed around for ten hours. I was certain they didn't have any shock absorbers.

Making these recordings is much more difficult than it appears. It is not just a matter of talking onto the tape. We have to check each sentence to make sure that the language helper understands the meaning and is saying it correctly in his language. For five days we worked hard from dawn until dusk. I was tired, but our language helper had blood-shot eyes and didn't know if he was coming or going.

Next, we headed to Bwanga. We waited for seven hours by the side of the road looking for any means of transport—lorries, tractors, busses. After a long wait, a postal truck came along. It was already packed with bodies and had no windows. Someone told us that a bus might pass at 2:00 a.m. so we decided to wait.

The bus arrived at 4:00 a.m. and we braced ourselves for another bumpy ride. After three hours we made an unexpected stop. A lady passenger gave birth to a baby girl. All the mamas got out and gave assistance. After 20 minutes the lady got on the bus with her newborn, and off we went. Everyone clapped and said it was a blessing. They told us that often the mother or baby didn't survive. After bouncing on those roads, I can understand why.

We praised God that we were able to make recordings in three languages of Tanzania before we returned to Nairobi, Kenya. Before I left I heard about another tribe that is virtually unreached. I want to get more information on them and make a trip down there. This means l-o-n-g-e-r bus trips. But it sure beats walking.

Waiting for God's Time

Rob Harris

SUDAN, NORTH AFRICA

When I walked into the Sudanese embassy in Nairobi, Kenya, and applied for my Sudanese visa, I knew from what people had told me that it wouldn't be easy to obtain. Nevertheless, I had an underlying assurance that God wanted me in Sudan to initiate a recording program that would make it possible for many tribal groups like the Mabaan to hear the Good News in their own languages.

Not long after my arrival in Nairobi, I learned that the archbishop of Sudan had a strong burden for evangelism and discipleship of the people in the southern part of Sudan. After corresponding with him for several months I was able to visit Sudan on a tourist visa and meet with him. He shared my burden for making recordings and willingly agreed to act as liaison with the government for obtaining a visa.

I went back to Nairobi to wait for my visa. A missionary working in Kenya informed me that there was not much chance of my getting a visa that way. "Try another way," he said. Another missionary with the gift of discouragement informed me that I would be carried out of Sudan in a box if I went in alone. These things drove me to pray more earnestly that God would open up the door. My heart went out in love to the tribes of Sudan.

While I waited, God gave me the opportunity to fly to Zaire (Congo) to make recordings in a number of languages. The first part of my trip was spent among the pygmies of the Ituri forest. We had traveled deep into the forest to record a dialect when our vehicle slid off the muddy road into a ditch.

So, here I was in the heart of Africa, at 3:30 a.m., with a group of pygmies pushing a car out of the ditch. Suddenly, my hometown of Hereford, England, seemed a long way away.

During that Zaire trip God enabled me to make recordings in 20 languages and dialects. The Africans who helped were enthusiastic. In one area, a man who was seriously ill and not expected to live insisted on climbing the hill where I had set up my makeshift studio. He wanted to help me with the recordings. He had a large vision for the way these materials could be used. This man is said to have led many thousands to the Lord during his evangelistic ministry. It was a privilege to work with him.

Back again to Nairobi and more waiting. Many days I lost heart and got discouraged. Doubts often crept in. Then one day a scrawled note arrived in the mail. It looked uninteresting and was hard to decipher. But it informed me that the Sudanese government had granted approval for me to work in their country. God had opened the door! The 18 months of waiting were over.

Why did the Lord let me wait so long? I believe it was so that I could make recordings in Kenya, Madagascar and Zaire. This gave me valuable experience as a new recordist. It also tested my faith and taught me that His ways are perfect – not always easy but always perfect. The time spent waiting on God gave me grounding in the Lord that I needed, because looking back on my first term on the field it was a struggle against the enemy all the way.

Satan sought to discourage me in many ways: bad news from home, personality conflicts, hardships, and the feeling at times of being totally alone. But God showed me that all the things He allowed to happen were to be used to shape my character and to change me into the likeness of His Son. Because of this I began to learn to praise Him in all things. To God what is important is not only what I am doing, but what He is doing in me. God is as interested in what I am as in the work that I do.

God also showed me that He is greater than any obstacle. He equips us and makes the way for His work to be carried out, and not even Satan can stand against it. So I praise God that He blessed His work, and through His enabling allowed me to make recordings for 74 language groups during my time in Africa.

God helped me adjust to the lifestyle in Sudan. On one occasion a bishop said that I was a real African the way I enthusiastically dug into eating goat's stomach and intestines with all ten fingers!

God proved to me that He is able to supply abundantly for all situations. Someone put a vehicle at my disposal, but it seemed impossible to find a source of gasoline in oil-starved Sudan. A Christian brother brought in five barrels from Kenya as a gift. He said that one of his priorities was to get me mobile because it was so important that recordings be made. What a blessing this cooperative attitude was to me. Truly God is able to make a way in the wilderness.

> *You can listen to the Mabaan language at:*
> *globalrecordings.net/en/language/907*

In the Presence of my Enemies

Colin Stott, Yopie Rattu

INDONESIA

When I arrived in Ambon, Indonesia, I found myself in the middle of a war. Muslim soldiers were shooting at Christians. I took cover next to a small food stall. The owner was scared. I told her not to be frightened and asked her to prepare some food for me. As I ate, she hid under the table while the shooting went on. Bullets passed over the roof. I was reminded of Psalms 23:5, "You prepare a table before me in the presence of my enemies."

An hour later, I boarded a fifteen-passenger boat to visit another town. As the boat was about to leave, another speedboat zoomed up to the dock. My cousins were in the boat. They had heard what was happening and were looking for me. So I got off my boat and joined them in theirs. This allowed another person to take my place on the first boat.

Both boats set off together. Suddenly, two speedboats came by and began shooting at the boat I had just left. All fifteen passengers were killed. I never found out why.

That's how things are going in Ambon. I plan to return there as more languages await the good news. The name of our Lord Jesus Christ be exalted and praised!

No More Secrets

Alex Shaw

INDIA - The Bhil Sansi

Alex Shaw rifled through his file of scripts. He and his wife Sybil were in India preparing to make recordings in another tribal language. The first lines of a script entitled 'A New Nature' caught his eye. "You can cut off a thief's hand, but the desire is still in his heart." Aha. An ideal message to record for a tribe of professional thieves.

Somewhere near us, thought Alex, that tribe is living – and no doubt employing their trade. It was the only available 'employment' and they did it with great gusto. No one trusted people from that tribe to work in their homes, their shops, their fields. This tribe was avoided. Their name? The 'Bhil Sansi.'

The Shaws prayed, "Father, lead us to this tribe for Jesus' sake." But no one, not even the local missionary, had the slightest clue as to their whereabouts. They only knew the result of visits from them. They didn't know it then, but the tribe was hiding right under their noses.

A national worker brought three men to the Shaws, thinking that they were the Hadair tribe of bone collectors. It wasn't until they began to casually chat through their interpreter that the light suddenly dawned. These people were not Hadairs. They were Bhil Sansi. What an opportune mistake. God had brought them to their very doorstep.

However, recording them was not going to be easy. The men let Alex and Sybil know they wouldn't cooperate until their tribal leaders would give permission. Alex went with the men. He was a little apprehensive, and prayed hard. Before too long, he returned accompanied by four Bhil Sansi men, and the village headman. They needed further reassurance as well as an understanding of the script 'A New Nature'. Alex and Sybil talked together at length and finally the men nodded, "Yes. It's true. Stealing is wrong, we know. We don't want to do it. But how can we stop?" They're taking the message personally. That's a good beginning.

Eventually the men were prepared to begin recording. With some hesitation the headman sat behind the microphone. Alex gave the first sentence to the interpreter. When they agreed on the translation, they practiced the wording until it was perfect.

Now the signal – "Go." Recording began. But, instead of speaking a few words as instructed, the headman went on and on. When he finally stopped, an astonished Alex said, "That wasn't what you practiced. What else did you say?"

"Oh," replied the headman, "we have to give some explanation first."

"Well, all right," countered Alex, not without suspicion. "Let's do it again. But leave all of the extra talk out this time. Just the one sentence." The headman nodded his agreement, but the same thing happened again. Alex stopped the recording until he could get to the bottom of this mystery.

Alex and Sybil listened patiently until the man's fears surfaced. The Shaws were strangers. What they were doing was even stranger. Didn't they know that the Bhil Sansi was a secret language? Why did they want to record it? The Bhil Sansi was a tribe of professional thieves. These recordings could be used against them. They were afraid. So what was the harm if the headman just described into the microphone a fight he'd had with another man? That couldn't get them into any trouble.

It was evident that this was not the right time for recording. Reluctantly, Alex and Sybil let the men return to their settlement, wondering if and how they would ever calm their fears and gain their confidence sufficiently to record God's message of forgiveness and love in their language. But God had given the

Shaws this burden for the Bhil Sansi. And He had led the Bhil Sansi men to them. They would continue to trust God to work out the difficulties.

A few days later, Victor, a national who had helped the Shaws on earlier occasions, arrived. After hearing the episode he said, "A few years ago a group of Bhil Sansi came to live in my village. I made friends with them, and then about six years ago they moved away. I wonder if they have joined the tribe in this nearby settlement. Let's find out."

Victor and the local missionary headed towards the settlement. The first man they met was one of those friends Victor had made long before.

The Bhil Sansi believe they are obligated to help friends in need. Victor was a friend and his friends, the Shaws, had a need. Therefore Victor's friend agreed to do the recording.

During the following days, confidence replaced fear. The Shaws' were able to record six messages in the Bhil Sansi language. They rejoiced in the answer to their prayers.

The recorded messages were shared with several Bhil Sansi groups. After several months, 14 tribal people believed on the Lord Jesus Christ and were baptized.

No more secrets.

You can listen to the Bhil Sansi language at:
globalrecordings.net/en/program/C16830

Not for the Fainthearted

Dan Rulison

Names have been changed for security purposes

In 1960, a man whom we'll name Abdul was sent by his government to study agriculture in the U.S. He was from a Muslim nation.

During his four years of study, he encountered Christians who led him to Christ. Fellow students from his country reported this and he was told to return home immediately. Abdul did graduate, but upon his return home he was arrested. Because he refused to recant, he was sentenced to death. His uncle, who was a military general, approached the authorities and persuaded them that convincing him to recant was a family matter. He was released to his uncle's custody.

During this time, Abdul was allowed to begin practicing the agricultural theory he had learned in the U.S. Because he did so well he quickly advanced until he became the national minister of agriculture. All the while he continued to secretly study the Bible.

His country was in turmoil for several years with an ongoing war. Then a radical party took control of the government. At that time Abdul was ill and visited another country to get treatment. The new radical leaders knew of his Christian sentiments and sent police to his home to kill him. His son and daughter-in-law and their infant were there and endured a terrible beating as the police tried to get information about their father's whereabouts. The baby died as a result and the police vowed to kill more family members if they did not cooperate.

Somehow the son and daughter-in-law, along with a few other family members, managed to escape the country. They joined their ill father and flew immediately to a place where they received political asylum.

For years Abdul had desired to share the Gospel in a relevant way with his own countrymen. He wondered how he could make audio recordings for them. Remarkably, he came into contact with a recordist from Global Recordings Network (GRN). Surely this was one of those divine appointments.

As a result, GRN was able to make recordings in his language. He and one of his daughters were the speakers. Abdul only agreed to do it after he was assured that their voices on the recordings would be well disguised. Even then, one of his other daughters who is now a refugee in a country neighboring his home, pleaded with him not to do the recording. She feared for her own safety.

This is not a job for the fainthearted.

Come Back Tomorrow

Allan Starling

Côte d'Ivoire - West Africa

People thrive on respect. And when you take it away, you also lose their cooperation. I learned this the hard way one humid afternoon at the international airport in Abidjan, Côte d'Ivoire (Ivory Coast) West Africa.

My orange boarding pass was tucked into my damp shirt pocket. Sweat trickled down my face while I tried to relax on the hard wooden waiting room bench. Without warning, the other passengers jumped up and moved toward the boarding gate. Through the window, I saw an aircraft taxi toward our gate. The hot African sun glinted off its silver skin. What's the hurry, people? We all have assigned seats. Relax. With the superior attitude of one who has been there and done that, I waited for the boarding announcement then sauntered up to join the end of the line.

That was my first mistake.

We were about to board when a uniformed official approached a few of us at the back of the line. He asked my name, glanced at his clipboard, and said, "May I see your boarding pass, sir? Thank you. Come with me please." He escorted six of us bewildered passengers to a counter a short distance from the gate. The man addressed us in French and my fellow passengers responded with loud indignant cries. I stood there wide-eyed, not understanding a word. Finally I yelled above the din, "Will somebody please tell me in ENGLISH what is going on"? Our man turned to me. "Sorry, sir. The plane is full. You will have to come back tomorrow."

How can they do this to me? I have people waiting in Freetown,

Sierra Leone. How do I contact them? Our little group continued to protest. Now I knew the reason for their concern, but that didn't make me feel any better. The official bowed politely. "If you need further help you will have to go to the airline office." That was a clever way to get rid of us. The official pointed down a corridor and our posse strode off. This time I made sure not to bring up the rear. We crowded into a neat but small office. The only occupant, a large African woman in a flowing green dress, looked up from her computer. Before she could speak, the posse fired their verbal shots. "We all have boarding passes and they wouldn't let us on the plane" ... "You can't do this to us" ... "Get us on another flight ..." Her back stiffened. Her eyebrows lowered. Her large brown eyes bored their way through the crowd as she barked, "There is no other plane. Come back tomorrow!"

A stream of angry protests broke the initial stunned silence. "You have to put us up in a hotel" ... "You have to make sure we are on the plane tomorrow" ... "We deserve compensation." But under that flowing dress she wore a virtual bulletproof vest. With a withering look at our now deflated troop, she outlined the situation.

"Today is today." She swept it aside with her large hand. "Tomorrow is tomorrow." Her fist banged on the desk. "And tomorrow we have other passengers." She glared at us with a look of finality. "We will seat them first."

"But I've been here a week," wined a stout man in a wrinkled business suit. She snorted.

I was the token American in the group, so had to say my piece. My best offering was a terse, "This isn't fair!" Her back stiffened a bit more.

We were fighting a losing battle. Even the colorful travel posters looked down from the walls and mocked us. We were going nowhere. Our ammunition was spent. We were done. At that moment, a soft spoken, inconspicuous, man in a gray suit emerged from the back of the group.

"Madam," his quiet pleading tone was the antithesis of anything I had heard to that moment. "Madam, you are the only one who can help us. We are at your mercy. We beg you to help us. Please."

At that, a transformation took place. Her back relaxed, her glare melted and I thought I caught the faintest suggestion of a smile. With just two words she announced the truce.

"That's better."

Make no mistake. Our lady was still in charge! But now she was our ally. She would use what authority she had to help us. "Give me your names. I'll see that you are on the plane tomorrow." Yes, we still had to come back the next day. No, the airline didn't put us up in a hotel. But as we stood watching, she called headquarters and told them she had six passengers that had to be given top priority on the next flight.

I was fortunate in that the missionary who dropped me off at the airport had given me a local coin with the advice, "Call me if you have a problem." As he picked me up to take me home for the night, he explained, "I heard a rumor that their larger airliner was out of commission so they are temporarily using a smaller craft. No wonder they were overbooked."

True to her word, our new champion saw to it that our little group was the first to board that next morning's flight. I surrendered the orange boarding pass and made for the silver aircraft. But my relief was tinged with guilt. I couldn't help wonder if our little band was about to take the seats of another group of unsuspecting passengers. I could only hope that in their beleaguered company was a soft-spoken unassuming savior who had already learned the importance of giving others the respect they needed, and deserved.

Field Recording Reminiscences

Valerie Deguchi

AFRICA

LIVING CONDITIONS

"What do you enjoy most about making the recordings?" a friend asked.

"When it is all over, going back to my home and having a bath," I replied. Usually, in the village, I would just have a bucket with which to bathe.

The huts normally had bed bugs and rats. I learned to sleep with my mouth shut, close my suitcase and put my shoes upside down because in the morning you never knew what you'd find inside them. But I could endure it because the people would move out of their homes in order for me to stay. I knew they gave their best, so how could I complain?

ANTIBIOTICS

I carry antibiotics with me because spiders and bugs like me and want to bite. Sometimes the bites get infected. Once, I went with a medical team of nationals to a small village in the bush where they were vaccinating. To my consternation, they used the same needle on about a hundred people. They don't have the resources to change needles for every person, so diseases such as AIDS spread rapidly.

While we were there, I got a bite and my leg swelled to over double its size and it hurt. "Do you want a shot of penicillin?" one of the medical team asked.

"No thank you," I said thinking of used needles, "I'd rather die this other way."

After that I always carried my own syringe.

THE HONORABLE GOAT

I've eaten a lot of local food. When you go to a village, the people will often slaughter a goat to honor you. But, they don't give you the meat. The foul-smelling intestines are the delicacy. I'd have to eat while holding my breath because that was the only way I could get it down.

Once I was with another missionary couple. As usual, the people slaughtered a goat and brought us the intestines. Green things were floating on top of the dish.

"Oh look, these people cook with herbs," said the other lady.

We blurted out laughing because we knew it wasn't herbs. It was the grass that they hadn't cleaned out from the intestines!

VISAS

I got off the plane in eastern Zaire; a place where law and order tends to depend on the whim of the official in charge. The customs officer said to me, "Your passport's not intact." "What do you mean it's not intact?" I said.

"You're here illegally."

"No I'm not."

"We're going to have to put you in jail," he said.

Of course there was no jail. I knew he was bluffing. He wanted me to pay some money but I wasn't going to. So I said "Okay. Do it," and stood there praying while he talked back and forth with his cronies and with the pastor who had come to meet me. Finally they decided, despite the pastor's protests, to put me under house arrest.

But then the pastor pointed out to them, "If you keep her you're going to have to feed her."

They let me go!

CARS

You never travel alone in a car because it's 'big-time stuff' to ride in a car. We always had people wanting to travel with us and it's difficult to explain to them that the car is full because "there's always room for one more."

The roads are very bad. We often had to make our own bridges with logs. At first, I would say, "I'm not crossing in the vehicle with the rest of you. I'm walking over." But then I thought, "If they are all killed, what will I do, way out here with no way to get back?" So I decided, "If we're going to go, we're all going to go together."

Divine Appointment

Allan Starling

MEXICO - The Mixtec Language

Robert Bloemendaal walked around the small Mixtec village in southern Mexico. He was carrying his recording equipment and looking for someone who spoke both Spanish and their particular dialect of the Mixtec language. People pointed him to a humble house and told him it was the best place to go. He knocked and called out, "Buenos Dias!"

A lady came to the door and Robert began explaining that he wished to find someone willing to help him record Bible messages. As he talked, he could see her eyes light up in amazement. She excused herself and came back in a few minutes with a cassette tape. He could tell from the label that it was a GRN recording. But how did she come to have it in her home?

The lady explained that two years before, she and her family had been in a migrant labor camp in Culiacan, Mexico—a town about 1,000 miles from their home. One evening a team came to the camp offering a cassette tape to each family. First they asked her what district she was from. Then they played a short message in several Mixtec dialects. (She didn't know there were recordings in 64 of those dialects.) After several tries she said, "Esa es mi idioma!"—that is my language!

One of the team members hurried away and soon came back with a cassette, which he presented to her. This was the first time she had received a recording in her very own heart language. She played it over and over listening intently to the Bible teachings. Moved by the message, she accepted Jesus as her Savior. When her husband and son came back from the fields, she played the messages to them, and they both asked Jesus to be their Savior.

Soon the harvesting was over, and the family moved back to their village. There was no church for them to attend and no other Christians in the village. All they had was the tape from GRN.

Fascinated, Robert listened as the lady told her story. Things were now bad in their village. There was no rain to water their meager crops. There was no work. And now both her husband and son were ill. What could they do? There was only one thing they knew. Before he knocked on that door in that small village, the family had prayed to the Lord and asked Him to send someone along to help and encourage them!

MAKING THE RECORDINGS

Most of us picture the typical recording studio as a comfortable, well insulated, soundproofed building with a huge console bristling with hundreds of little knobs, operated by a technician.

Not so at Global Recordings Network.

Once the language has been identified, the field recordist has to travel to where the speakers live. His next job is to find the necessary bilingual language helpers. No easy task. Equally challenging is the exercise of finding the most culturally relevant messages and stories to record. Then it's time to set up the equipment. This in itself is a challenge. Imagine landing in a primitive village with no electricity and huts with thin bamboo walls. How do you, for instance, shut out the noises of chickens cackling, children crying, and curious onlookers exclaiming in wonder at the unusual proceedings? How do you explain the process to people who have never seen a recorder or heard their language being spoken by a box?

The machines used in the "Recording the Wakindiga" story were a far cry from today's compact, light equipment that produces crisp recordings. But the present field recordists face the same challenge of performing a high-tech job in a low-tech environment. Their motto—Telling the Story of Jesus in Every Language—has never changed.

Recording the Wakindiga

A continuation of Finding the Wakindiga

Sanna Barlow - Light is Sown

TANZANIA - EAST AFRICA
The Wakindiga Language

Early Monday morning, at the mission station in Isanzu, Tanzania, Joy, Ann and I waited on tiptoe for Bob Ward's car to return. He had gone to pick up the three Wakindiga pygmies who came at the chief's request to speak on the recordings. When Bob returned, we at first thought he was alone. But he opened the back door of the car, and out stepped three little men—bronze-brown, wide-eyed and shy, but not without their bows and arrows. The old chief...a Mzee...reached out his rough little hand with a Swahili greeting, "Jambo, Mama."

I wondered what these men thought of the three 'mamas' bursting with squeals of delight. We had worked and prayed so hard to contact the pygmies, and here they were.

Bob and Edythe Ward from Isanzu mission helped in the recording process. It took at least 48 hours of solid labor. We divided into two teams. Edythe interpreted from English to Swahili for one group while Bob and African Pastor Paulus provided a clear and accurate translation from English through Swahili and Kinisanzu into Wakindiga. In turn, the Mzee taught the young man seated beside him the lines he was to speak into the box. As he himself spoke into the mike, the Mzee taught the box what to say, wagging his forefinger to lend a schoolmaster's authority to the lesson. No wonder the recorder usually recited correctly!

We were not sure if the gracious old man understood that this was actually his own voice on the playback. It seemed he was simply concerned that the recorder learn its lesson well. Now and then he would agree to our suspicion that the box had made a kosa kidogo, a little mistake. A quick correction always evoked his special little nod of commendation and "mzuri sana, very good."

The work proceeded into the progressively warmer hours of the day. At times the boy squirmed in his seat. Several times the helper behind the microphone in the other team threatened to go on strike. "Why do we talk more about God? We're finished with Him." And at another moment of exasperation, "Why do I talk about God? I don't know Him." Imagine the ordeal it must have been for a child of the forest to be caged like this, forced to sit in a chair, perhaps for the first time in his life, and to think. How excruciating. On the other hand, the Mzee's sweet grace and patience never lagged, no matter how tried he was.

The going became extremely difficult during those hot sleepy hours after lunch. Following a feast of meat supplied by the missionary, their brains appeared to take a well-deserved siesta. A thought would slip into oblivion before it could be repeated into the microphone. There was the will to do, but the nguvu, the strength, was gone. So we presented the old man and the dozing boy with a harmless white pill (Anacin tablet) and a cup of water.

"For you, Mzee. It is dawa." Dawa is medicine, a word of charm in Africa.

"Kwa nini, Mama."—For what, Mama?"

"Kwa nguvu sana."—For pep."

A torrent of Swahili came from the Mzee which Bwana Bob relayed. "He says, 'Mama, what will I do when you are not here to give me dawa.'" Everybody laughed.

The dawa helped and progress was made on the taping of the story called "Tell me about Jesus." As we looked out across the lawn of the mission house, we could see the shadows lengthen. Time sped by while our work on the dialog plodded slowly, slowly along. We followed the script line by line, adapting it when the speakers could not express the words in their language.

Boy: Father, tell me the story that begins, "In the beginning God made all things. He made the world, the stars."

Mzee: The sun, the moon; He made the trees, the birds and animals. Afterward He made the first man and the first woman.

Boy: And they were good absolutely. They loved to obey and please God.

Mzee: Yes. But then one day Satan, the evil one, tempted them to disobey God. They listened to Satan and obeyed his words. When they did this, they turned away from God. They disobeyed God's good commandments.

Boy: Ahhh... and then they were no longer good, as before. Is this not true?

Mzee: It is true. And afterward, all people born on earth have in the same way walked in crooked ways. Not one has perfectly obeyed God. Yet God felt great pity for all the people of the world.

Boy: Did not God leave them, then, after they chose to go their own way?

Mzee: No, son, the Book of God tells us that God did not leave or forget them. His pity for them was great, because He knew that all who walked in the ways of darkness would go to the place of darkness when they died. And God did not want any of them to perish.

Boy: And so, what did God do then?

Mzee: You know the story, my son, and the words which say, "For God so loved ..."

Boy: "For God so loved the world that he gave his only begotten son, that whosoever believeth in him should not perish, but have everlasting life."

It was interesting to see the Mzee learn this immortal passage—John 3:16—and as he learned a phrase he and his forefinger taught it faithfully to the boy who then spoke it to the box with confidence.

Just here, the taping half-finished, Bwana Bob was called away. A Muslim sub-chief was trying to make trouble because of our work with the Wakindiga. Everything came to a standstill while we waited. It could ruin everything, Jean Ward told us, if the Muslim chief should decide to outlaw the recordings and forbid their distribution. This was another of those incidents which emphasize the conflict inherent in every advance into unclaimed territory. It was a part of the inevitable undertow, a reminder to never take a prize for granted; to never be careless as though the adversary slept.

We clung to Paul's reminder, "Don't worry about anything; instead, pray about everything. Tell God what you need, and thank him for all he has done" (Phil. 4:6).

We sharpened our blades on the word from Isaiah 54:17, "No weapon turned against you will succeed. You will silence every voice raised up to accuse you. These benefits are enjoyed by the servants of the Lord; their vindication will come from me. I, the Lord, have spoken."

After a while Bob returned. The sub-chief was pacified by the knowledge that the head chief had himself approved and aided this procedure.

You can listen to the Wakindiga language at:
globalrecordings.net/en/program/C02291

This story is continued in The Wakindiga Listen

Milestones
Keeping up with Technology

Allan Starling

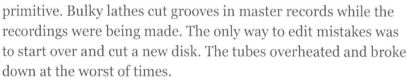

When Joy Ridderhof started out on the recording journey 75 years ago, she did have had the word 'technology' in her vocabulary. But as it turned out, her simple but brilliant idea of using phonograph records took her and her young ministry down a path that relied on increasingly sophisticated high-tech equipment and procedures that were used to reach low-tech people.

By today's standards, the first recording equipment was clumsy and primitive. Bulky lathes cut grooves in master records while the recordings were being made. The only way to edit mistakes was to start over and cut a new disk. The tubes overheated and broke down at the worst of times.

The early equipment was hard enough to use in a comfortable, air-conditioned studio. But they needed to record on location. This meant toting heavy machines and generators around the world and using them in hot dusty environments, exposing the equipment to even more hazards. At times the machine failed in the middle of a recording session. Joy would remove the vacuum tubes, lick them, pray, rejoice, put everything back, and the machine would start working! But as primitive as these recording devices were, they produced recordings that changed people's lives!

It was a huge milestone when a staff member, Herman Dyk, was able to make the first-ever portable tape recorder—the Minidyk. Then in 1958 Joy heard about a rugged tape recorder about to come on the market. The price was high, and reporters and television newsmen were falling over each other to obtain models. Undaunted she started to pray. The Nagra turned out to be a very reliable GRN workhorse for years to come. (See "MILESTONES: The Nagra Story.")

Another challenge was playing the records in thousands of locations where there was no electricity. Stuart Mill, the Director of Gospel Recordings Australia, invented and produced an ingenious mechanical hand-wound record player called the Phonette. This machine was reproduced in steel, plastic and wood and sent all over the world. An even simpler cardboard record player was perfected by the staff in Los Angeles and named the CardTalk.

A significant landmark was evidenced by the switch from records to audiocassettes. Once again, Australia answered the challenge and invented a hand-cranked cassette player. It looked like a regular tape player, but a small generator supplied electricity to the motor as long as the crank was turned, giving new meaning to the term 'batteries not included.' Unlike records that had to be centrally manufactured, the audiocassettes could be duplicated anywhere in the world.

Digital technology provided a new milestone for GRN. Now the same Gospel messages and songs in over 6,000 languages and dialects are available in a whole range of media from CDs and DVDs to MP3s. Programs in over 5,000 of these languages can be listened to or downloaded from GRN's web site. GRN Australia has come through again with a rugged hand-cranked MP3 player (the Saber) that can be used anywhere.

As we work overtime to keep up with technology, we look to the Lord to show us the next milestone. The possibilities are endless, but the goal remains the same—telling the story of Jesus in every language.

MiniDyk

78 rpm Records

Phonette Record Player

Messenger Cassette Player

Saber Mp3 Player

A Time to Improvise

Told to Allan Starling

In 1990, Jon Rulison was on a recording assignment in Cameroon, Africa. GRN called him a Field Recordist. But this title didn't adequately describe his responsibilities. He was part missionary, part linguist, and part technician. In his missionary role, he would like to have spent a lifetime with each group he visited. But he needed to move on to others who had not heard the message of salvation. In his linguist role, he would like to have taken the time to learn each given language. But he had to rely on interpreters. In his role as a technician, he did not have the luxury of professional recording artists or ideal recording conditions. His job was to study a given language group, assess the most culturally relevant Gospel stories and messages to record, and find the best available language helpers. He then had to overcome technical hurdles, make audio recordings of evangelistic and basic Christian teaching, then repeat the process with the next group.

A missionary who knew the local trade language transported Jon from one language group to the next. They discovered that the missionary's car would serve as a good studio. The car's upholstery and uneven surfaces provided suitable studio qualities because they reduced echoes. Jon set up his recording equipment on the back seat. The missionary sat in front with the language helper and discussed, via the trade language, what was to be recorded. After the language helper had practiced a sentence or passage in his native tongue, Jon gave a signal and turned on the recorder. They repeated the process until the entire story or message was recorded. In this way, Jon was able to complete recordings in several languages.

Then they arrived at a small village, and the missionary introduced a man who was the only one willing to speak on the recordings in his language. There was just one problem. He was blind. How would Jon, who was in the back seat, signal him when it was time to speak? He needed both hands to operate the recorder, so could not reach over and tap him.

Jon sat with his recording equipment in the back as usual. The missionary in the driver's seat watched him through the rear-view mirror. When he saw Jon's nod, he tapped the speaker next to him on the leg. Several messages were recorded successfully using this method.

When he moved on to another area of Cameroon, Jon didn't even have an automobile studio. In a remote village he was shown to a house that was being built. Would this work? The walls were concrete and the rooms empty. He clapped his hands and the sharp sound reverberated around the room. With a quick prayer for help, Jon shook his head. The nationals led him next to the back of the village where an unattractive mud-walled structure was also in the process of being constructed. The thatch roof absorbed sound well. The mud floors and unfinished open windows reduced echo. Once again, God had provided the perfect studio for his lonely recordist.

Jon wished he had been able to spend more time with each language group. He often wondered if his unorthodox recordings had been effective. But he had moved on, and had no way of evaluating the results. Years later, a professor and some students from California visited Cameroon. They took with them Jon's GRN recordings. They attempted to explain the Gospel message to the people, using the trade language. The listeners appeared to be very unresponsive. Next day, the professor played the recordings Jon had made years before. This caused an immediate transformation. Faces brightened, all talking stopped, and eyes were riveted on the player.

Yes, recording conditions had been far from ideal and the speakers were not recording artists. Yet people sat up and took notice when they heard Jon's improvised recordings of messages from God's word spoken by their tribal people in their own language. Hearts were stirred and many turned to the Lord.

The Perils of Recording

Kish Bai

NIGERIA, WEST AFRICA - The Kukele Language

It's not easy to make GRN recordings. Those who try face many barriers. The geographic barrier places some language groups far from the beaten path, and face to face with physical dangers. The political barrier makes it difficult to enter some countries. The language barrier forces the recordist to search for bilingual language helpers. The manpower barrier means that some groups have to wait. The prejudice barrier makes it difficult to find cooperative helpers. In Nigeria GRN field recordists face most of these barriers at one time or another. But the most dangerous is the religious barrier.

These types of perils are part of the daily routine for many of our recordists. The GRN recording team from Northern Nigeria that travelled to the Kukele people in Cross River State, Southern Nigeria, was no exception. Only, this time it was a problem in reverse.

Their recording trip was accompanied by multiple breakdowns. The vehicle's fan failed and caused the head gasket to blow. The exhaust system required repairs, the starter motor failed, and then the drive shaft. They praised God for a mechanic's help.

They arrived in the village on a Saturday and were pleased to discover a women's meeting taking place in the church. A good initial contact. But when the women saw from their license plate that they came from northern Nigerian, they jumped to the conclusion that they were terrorists. Someone ran to warn the pastor that terrorists had come to bomb the church and kill them. The pastor immediately left the church and hid.

To allay the people's fears, the team played a GRN recording of some Gospel music from a loudspeaker on their vehicle. But the women saw this as a ruse by terrorists to disguise themselves as missionaries and to gain their trust. The team insisted on seeing the pastor, but the ladies were unwilling to help. Finally the pastor's daughter led the team to his house, very much against the wishes of the group, and provided chairs so that they could sit outside and await the pastor's return.

While they waited, the team was attacked by a poisonous snake and managed to kill it before anyone was harmed. Much later the pastor summoned up courage to go home. The first man he saw was the team's guide, a former Bible college classmate. The pastor ran and hugged him. The women looking on were amazed. It was much like a scene from a movie.

The pastor took the team around and introduced them to the other churches. He also scouted for language helpers to assist with the recording and found several willing to participate. Within two hours the pastor received a call from his supervisor saying that he had been informed that the pastor was harboring terrorists. Thankfully, this interruption did not stop the work.

The next day, Sunday, the team was given time in the service to introduce the ministry of GRN and to reassure the people that they were not Muslim terrorists. Everyone was pleased, and the recordings were made.

It is sobering to realize that so many people live in fear of terrorist attacks. Churches are bombed and Christians are killed in Nigeria with monotonous regularity. It takes courage to even attend church in much of Nigeria; our GRN workers are Nigerian nationals working under very adverse circumstances. But they do their job willingly in order to tell the story of Jesus in the languages of their countrymen.

To listen to a recording of the Kakele language, go to this link: globalrecordings.net/en/program/C10171

Milestones
The Nagra Story

Allan Starling

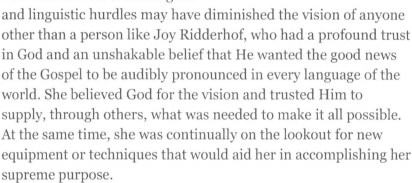

An organization like GRN could logically have been founded by a language expert or a technician. Instead it grew up around a woman who possessed neither of these seemingly essential qualities. But the immense technological and linguistic hurdles may have diminished the vision of anyone other than a person like Joy Ridderhof, who had a profound trust in God and an unshakable belief that He wanted the good news of the Gospel to be audibly pronounced in every language of the world. She believed God for the vision and trusted Him to supply, through others, what was needed to make it all possible. At the same time, she was continually on the lookout for new equipment or techniques that would aid her in accomplishing her supreme purpose.

The Nagra story is a case in point. The highly sensitive, lightweight yet remarkably robust tape recorder came on the market in 1958. It was in great demand by the media industry and the price was high. But Joy was undeterred. She prayed earnestly. In the end, her inconspicuous little organization, unheard of by the national mass media, was receiving a steady supply of the coveted machines while the newsmen waited impatiently for months.

This is how it came about. On Joy's first trip to England she visited Livingston Hogg, an electronics consultant. He told her, "If you want a really good battery-operated recording machine, the best in the world will be coming on the market soon. It's just the thing you need. It's called the Nagra. The inventor is a Swiss man named Kudelsky."

In her typical fashion, Joy immediately fastened on the information.

Right from the start the recording machine had been the mechanical key to her work. Upon it everything depended. All the careful preparation of scripts, all the arrangements with interpreters, all the arduous travel produced no recordings if the machine went wrong. She was always on the alert to learn of new and improved methods, of models that were lighter to carry, easier to work, less liable to breakdowns. She made a note of the Nagra, and the name of the inventor, but could do nothing else except pray, as she frequently did, for better machines.

Joy had arranged to stay in Switzerland for a few days on her way to Africa. The Nagra was on her mind as well as the name of its inventor. She did not know where he lived, but prayed that God would lead her to him. Her host not only knew where Mr. Kudelsky lived, but was personally acquainted with him and offered to arrange a meeting. A short time later she found herself sitting and talking with him.

"It isn't completed yet," Kudelsky told her. "It must be foolproof, able to stand up to very hard wear. We are planning to test it by dropping it from the air by parachute. It'll be mainly used by reporters." The matter of distributors came up, and Joy suggested Livingston Hogg for England. "Oh, I've got twenty people who would take it on," the inventor replied. Then he asked casually, "How many machines will you want?"

She had not expected the question. With her intimate and varied experience of recording machines, she knew that this new one could have a transforming effect on the work of the field recordists. But she also knew how much each machine cost—approximately the price of a new automobile.

"How many machines will you want?" The question remained suspended in air, waiting for an answer, and she knew she must say something.

"Twenty-four," she replied. Yet, on the strength of her bank balance she was in no position to order even one. Here she was talking in terms of the equivalent of a fleet of 24 new cars. The words were out before she had time to think, based on no wise assessments of her own. When the precious and rare Nagra recorders appeared one by one, with eager buyers clamoring to obtain them, those two words 'twenty-four' formed the basis on which the mission could claim to have placed an order which put it high on the priority list of customers to be supplied. And since Livingston Hogg was, in the end, appointed distributor of the Nagra in England, he was in a good position to ensure that the order was fulfilled.

Today, thousands of open-reel tapes that were originally recorded on those Nagra machines have been digitally remastered. The life-giving message they captured in countless languages still goes out, telling the story of Jesus.

- Making the Recordings -

One of Those Aha! Moments
A testimony from the Amazon

Colin Stott

Names have been changed for security purposes

It's always the same. Whether stepping off a plane onto a grass airstrip or climbing from a canoe onto a muddy riverbank, the first hours entering a village are always UFO time for me. I feel like a green alien with squinty eyes, smiling politely at the strangers who have come to witness my arrival. How do we ever get from zero to friends with people who are so different? But somehow the ice gets broken,  disparities of language and culture are reduced, friendships sprout and we get to a place where we can laugh and cry together. That's an amazing gift from God.

I experienced this all over again with the Buntaba people.

Sabatao was our neighbor in the village, and a main language helper for recording. We rigged up a makeshift recording studio in the plantation and worked hard during those three weeks. How we appreciated our brother's heart and the sparkle in his eye as he translated. Sabatao shared with us how he and his people felt sad about the prolonged absence of dear missionary friends who had lived with them off and on over the past fifteen years. The people were heavy hearted, not knowing if or when their teachers and pastors would return.

We began recording a series of chronological Bible messages, from creation through the fall of man, God's promise to Abraham, Jesus' birth, death and resurrection. Sabatao didn't know the story of Acts chapter two, so we explained to him the promise Jesus made to his friends before he left them – that he would send another Helper, the Spirit of truth, who would be with them forever (John 14:16,17). The disciples, too, must have felt pretty sad and discouraged after their dear friend/teacher/pastor left them.

That's when it hit me just how much those missionaries had been Jesus to the Buntaba people. In the same way, you and I are Jesus to the world around us. It also struck me how this promise of God-with-us pronounced so long ago still speaks so very personally today.

It impacted Sabatao too. We always pray that a language helper can get beyond just translating and really speak the message with conviction. Sabatao went on to repeat those words of comfort, telling his people the story of the Holy Spirit's arrival and His continued presence and help in the lives of believers today.

This was one of those moments that encourages me in my work.

Gaining a Passion for Souls

Eipeen Huang

MEXICO - The Pame Language

We had a tough time recording messages for the Pame Indians in Mexico. Their language has not yet been written down. This is where recordings can be so useful for bringing the truth of Jesus Christ to those who desperately need Him.

The village we visited was very troubled and resistant. Adultery, drunkenness and deception ran rampant. We battled humidity, exhaustion and fleas—I had over 300 bites.

For a month, I'd been trying to arrange these recordings. My search for a contact led me to a Bible translator for the Pame. He wanted to help but had too many other commitments. I was dismayed. But in my state of worry the Lord had me examine my motives.

Did I want to record in order to have something to tell my supporters – or because I genuinely cared about the Pame? I'm ashamed to admit that my motives were not 100 percent pure. I confessed this and asked the Lord to give me His passion for Pame souls.

That night I had a hard time sleeping, but the Lord put two names in my mind; Bashan and Zerubbabel. I didn't remember much about them, so I got out of bed and looked up their references.

Bashan was the land conquered during Moses' time and given to the tribes who stayed on the east side of the river Jordan while the rest lived over in the Promised Land. It made me think of the Pame Indians. They're like those who have stayed apart from the rest, left behind by the main culture.

Then I looked up Zerubbabel. It was to him that God said, "Not by might, nor by power, but by My Spirit." All I could do was thank the Lord for His promises, and then drift peacefully off to sleep.

Next morning, I called the missionary again. He promised to rethink the situation. The same night he emailed me that he sensed the Lord wanted us to make plans to record.

Praise God that we now have Christian recordings for the Pame. I am certain God has special plans for these people because of the way He so carefully arranged every detail.

You can listen to the Pame language at:
globalrecordings.net/en/language/4861

How much is it Worth?

Ann Sherwood - Light is Sown

SUDAN - NORTH AFRICA

I was setting up to make recordings at the leper hospital in Nyakma, Sudan, Africa. My studio was the little church at the edge of the colony, built by the loving hands of the lepers themselves. The recorder was placed in front of the platform, and hour after hour we recorded, with a small 'congregation' sitting on the board benches in front of us, enjoying every word whether they understood the language or not.

One young fellow with only stubs for hands and feet always sat on the front bench. But as the hours wore on, his strength would fail, and he would first sit on the gravel floor, leaning on the board behind him. When he could no longer sit, he would curl up on the floor, but his enjoyment was obviously so keen that he couldn't bear to leave.

The next day we were recording his language, and the beaming face in front of us showed unusual appreciation of the song we were recording. Then I played it back. Suddenly the joy was too great for him. He took the corner of the dirty gray cloth slung over his shoulder, and between teeth and stumps of hands, he extricated a precious, long-preserved penny. Then in ecstasy he hobbled toward me, extending his offering in those fingerless stubs - his all. I was reminded of earlier Christians of whom it was written, "They are being tested by many troubles, and they are very poor. But they are also filled with abundant joy, which has overflowed in rich generosity (2 Cor. 8:2)".

Delivering The Recordings

On the lower level of the GRN building in Temecula, California, you can see thousands of recorded tapes representing more languages than can be found in any one place in the world. The GRN website servers in the USA and Australia hold multiple terabytes of audio in thousands of languages—all telling the story of Jesus in a culturally relevant way.

But of course, these recordings are useless unless someone who speaks the language has an opportunity to listen to them. Oral learners obviously can't write and request the recordings or download them. The mission's small staff can't be everywhere, so GRN makes the recordings available to missionaries, national pastors, Christian churches—in fact, to anyone who wants to give the speaker of another language an opportunity to hear the Gospel message. Recordings can also be downloaded free of charge from the GRN website.

Light is for Sharing

Wightman Weese

NIGER, WEST AFRICA - The Hausa Language

"Nails for her bowl covers?" my wife asked. "What do you suppose she wants?"

Yelwa, the wiry little widow, turned to me and smiled. She repeated it to me, "K'usar fai-fai." She tried again, "You know, nails for the bowl covers that tell people about Jesus."

The light broke. 'Nails.' She wanted phonograph needles! The bowl covers – well, the Gospel records did look a little like the round thatched bowl covers the local women made.

Several months before, we had given her a cleverly designed phonograph that could be turned by spinning the finger around in a little crank-like device sitting on the top of the recording. Yelwa was Hausa, but from her milk chocolate skin, she looked as if she could have been part Fulani also. We had given her a whole series of Hausa and Fulani recordings of Gospel presentations.

While I was back in the house looking for the needles, she explained to my wife that there was a Fulani village about six miles from our town. She had decided to visit a woman she had met. It was at the medical clinic we ran on the edge of the Sahara Desert in southern Niger Republic.

Late that afternoon we heard her weak call at the back door again. This time she brought another request. Typically, she went through long greetings before she got around to the real purpose of her visit. She wanted to know if my wife Priscilla could come with her sometime the next week.

"Is there someone there you want me to meet?" my wife asked. A quick nod of her head and a sucking in of her breath confirmed her request.

"There are seven women," she continued. "When I turned the 'bowl cover' for them, they said they wanted to know Yesu Almasihu (Jesus the Savior).

Yelwa's words made me think of another widow in the Bible. One day Jesus sat in the temple court and watched a widow, I think someone very much like Yelwa. He saw two tiny copper coins go into the horn that collected gifts from the worshippers. Many gifts were dropped in that day, but there was something special about her gift. Jesus said, "This poor widow has put in more than all; for all these out of their abundance have put in offerings for God, but she out of her poverty has put in all the livelihood that she had" (Luke 21:3,4).

This was Yelwa, the dried up little widow who often sat by our house and struggled to read even one verse from her Hausa Bible. She came often, but seemed to learn slowly. This was the old widow everyone had given up on—too old to find another husband, and almost too old to scratch out a little farm with her son-in-law, the pastor.

But she could still sit in her little grass hut on moonless nights and think about villages six miles away. At night she listened to hard-blowing rains pounding away on the thatched roof her son-in-law helped buy for her tiny dwelling. Snakes and scorpions sometimes found their way into her rolled up mat that was her bed. But somewhere in the tiny hut, among her handful of belongings, in some dry spot, the stack of dark bowl covers were carefully stored. With them, safely tied up in a little piece of cloth, were the half-dozen needles I had given her, the 'nails' that scratched out an ageless message of love and life.

Looking Inward: Light kept inside our hearts would be as futile as Yelwa's record player if she kept it hidden away in a dark corner of her hut. Even with the little light she had been given, this frail old saint knew that light was meant to be shared.

Looking Outward: The village was six miles away, but it called Yelwa like the voice the Apostle Paul heard in the night, calling him to Macedonia to help them. God doesn't always speak in audible tones to call us to those who need the light, but we must ask ourselves the question: "Would the ears of my heart be open to hear the call if it came?"

You can listen to the Hausa language at:
globalrecordings.net/en/program/C74543

A Muslim Helps

Patrick K.

MOROCCO, NORTH AFRICA

It's one thing to make recordings of the Gospel message. It's another to deliver them into the hands of the listeners. In some countries it is difficult. In Morocco, it could be dangerous. For every one million Muslims there are 150 Evangelicals. According to Voice of the Martyrs, "All Christian activity is carefully monitored by the government. Although talking about Christ is legal, proselytism and converting from Islam to Christianity are illegal. Muslims who convert to Christianity may face severe punishment. They endure ostracism from their families, loss of employment and imprisonment for their faith. Anti-Christian sentiment is common in the media. Between 2010 and 2013, Morocco deported at least 135 foreign Christians for proselytism. The government justified the deportations by claiming the Christians posed a threat to the state." All of the above makes the following story about the visit of two Australian Christians to Morocco even more amazing.

We took some GRN tapes and other materials on our trip into Morocco. We wanted to go to some of the remote villages, so we hired a local Berber Muslim man as a guide. While we were walking to the first village, the guide asked my friend what he was listening to through his earphones. He replied, "A praise tape."

"What's that?" the guide asked.

"Have a listen," my friend said. So he did. After a while I said, "Let's let him listen to a GRN Gospel tape." This was in his dialect. So we put that tape in the Walkman and continued on our way. Soon he said, "This is good. This is very good!"

When we got to the first village there were four men who knew our guide. They asked, "What are you doing?" He replied, "Hey, listen to this tape. It's very good!" He gave the earphones to each one to let them listen. The tape starts with Abraham and leads up to where it explains the Gospel. They all seemed to be enjoying it, so I said to the guide, "Can I give them each a tape?" He agreed, so I did.

Pretty soon the mullah walked up and asked what was going on. I thought, "Uh, oh, we're in trouble now." The guide told him, "We're listening to a tape in our language; here listen." So the mullah listened and said, "That's OK."

So we went on to the next village. Another friend of the guide asked what he was listening to, and the guide said, "Here, listen. It's in our language." I asked if I could give this fellow a cassette. The guide had listened to both sides of the tape twice by that time. He said, "Sure. It's good."

After listening, the man asked if I had something more. I had two copies of the Jesus film in their local dialect, so I said he could have one of them. He said, "Could I have two? I'm going to my in-laws in a village about four hours up the mountain and I'll show them the movie then leave one with them."

So, though this man was not even a Christian yet, he helped us get the Gospel into four villages!

We Can Understand

Alain Normand

CAMEROON, WEST AFRICA - The Bafek Language

Godswill Chongsi, a field recordist from the GRN base in the Cameroons, West Africa, gripped the wheel of our Nissan Patrol vehicle. He maneuvered slowly from one side of the narrow path to the other, trying to avoid the deep ruts. His guide, Jean Ndongo sat beside him and pointed the way. A third member of the party and I sat in the back and tried to enjoy the tropical landscape as we jolted along.

We were headed for the Bafek tribe, sixty miles north of Yaounde. Our goal was to place cassettes with evangelism messages into the hands of the people. As we slowly got closer, I wondered, would we receive a friendly welcome or be chased out of town?

I soon found out. We greeted the chief of the village, and he invited us to set up our equipment in a large community house. Soon more than 100 people of all ages arrived.

Jean Ndongo didn't know the tribe's language, so he addressed the crowd in the local trade language, which many understood. First he asked how much they knew of the Bible. Almost nothing. So he told them several Bible stories starting with Noah. After speaking of Jesus and his grace, Jean put a cassette in a hand-crank player and played Bible messages recorded in the tribe's own language, Bafek. The crowd was astonished to hear their language and quivered with excitement. An old man called out "We can all understand."

When Jean stopped the tape, he announced that copies of the

cassette would be offered to all who had players. They could take them home and hear the stories over and over again. The four of us started to place the little 'missionaries' into the hands of the people, but they crowded around us and anxiously grabbed for the packages. Soon all the cassettes were gone. People proclaimed their disappointment as they realized that there weren't enough for everyone. Jean promised that he would bring more when he travelled to a nearby village the next week.

When I finally got to bed late that night I was tired, but sleep was hard in coming. I kept seeing images of people in this remote village listening for the very first time in their lives to the Good News in their own language. I saw hands eagerly reaching out for recordings. Then I thought about other people in other towns who were still waiting.

You can listen to the Bafek language at:
globalrecordings.net/en/language/2888

Wrong Number?

Sandy Milligan

ROMANIA

I received a phone message asking me to return a call. All they left was a name and a phone number. I called the number and was requested to leave a numeric message on someone's pager.

About 20 minutes later I answered the phone and a gal said, "Someone paged me from this number." I asked if she had any idea what the nature of the call might be so I could connect her with the right department. She had no clue. Then I remembered that I had paged someone, a man's name, and I asked if she could hold while I checked to see if the number was hers.

When I got back to her I realized that I had transposed two of the numbers in the area code. So instead of calling my contact in Colorado I was calling a stranger in Alaska!

As I started to apologize, she said, "Can you tell me again the name of your company?" When I said "Gospel Recordings," she was overjoyed! She was a missionary home on furlough and knew of our mission. In fact, she was wondering how to contact us because a group from her church was going to Romania this summer! She then proceeded to order Romanian cassettes and several Gypsy languages for their trip.

When I finally made the correct call to the fellow in Colorado, he too had an exciting order for materials—but that's another story.

Crazy or Obedient?

Colin Stott

TIBET, CHINA

Stephanie Vernon, a little lady in her fifties, was typing address labels in the office of a Christian ministry in California when the Lord told her to go and witness to the Dalai Lama, the god-king of Tibet.

Some thought she must be crazy since she had no finances and was suffering from a kidney disease. But she was convinced that God wanted her to reach Tibetans with the Gospel.

Stephanie left for India with just a few hundred dollars in her purse, a round trip ticket, and a sixty-day tourist visa.

Those 60 days turned into 20 years of ministry among Tibetan refugees in several countries along the southern border of Tibet. During that time she visited almost all of the Buddhist monasteries in the region, giving out New Testaments to the monks. And she did meet with the Dalai Lama—several times.

Years ago, we were privileged to supply this dear servant of God with a record player and some phonograph records. She wrote: "I lugged that little player and records over the Himalayas and grinded the thing until my arm became numb. Because I played it so much, I wore out the needles, so I really hoarded the spare needles as if they were made of gold. I don't believe that I missed one Tibetan Camp. Eventually, I donated the player and records to one of the Tibetan monasteries—my precious little record player, which had become so very dear to me through the years. Without it, I could not have preached the Gospel to the hundreds and hundreds of Tibetan refugees."

Praise God for all the Tibetans who have heard of Christ because recordings were made in their own language, and for people like Stephanie who followed God in obedience.

Ismail Meets the Good Shepherd

Colin Stott

MEXICO - The Purepecha Language

Twelve-year old Ismail was cold and hungry. It had rained steadily all night and he had sheltered in a cave. His alcoholic father had sold him into a type of slavery. He never went to school and received no wages for his work as a shepherd. He barely existed on handouts of tortillas and beans.

He sat on a large stone with his sombrero and serape, the sheep scattered over the hills, and the beautiful pine trees strewn over the volcanic landscape. On the dirt road below, a vehicle slowly wound its way towards his village of San Lorenzo. He saw that the driver was of light complexion. Suddenly, an inner voice told him to run and stop the car. He had never dared to stop a car, much less with a gringo at the steering wheel. He reached the road ahead of the car and waved it to a stop. He found it hard to make himself understood because he spoke only a few words of Spanish. The driver, a missionary, guessed that he was cold and hungry so heated up some food for him on a small fire.

While Ismail ate, the missionary pulled a player from his trunk and sorted through a selection of recordings in various languages. He played short selections in Popoluco, Mazateco, Mixteco, Mayo, and Nahuatl, but Ismail could only shake his head. Then the box spoke in Purepecha. His language! He listened intently as the voice said, "I am the good shepherd...My sheep hear my voice, and I know them, and they follow me, and I give unto them eternal life, and nobody shall pluck them out of my hand (:)."

In his limited Spanish, Ismail implored, "Let me hear it again," and again, and again, until he had memorized the life-changing words. As the Spirit of God gave witness to his spirit that he was now a son of God, a new life began.

The missionary paid the boy's owners a few pesos to buy him out of slavery and took him into his family. Ismail grew in God's grace and in due time won his father to the Lord. He wanted to be a spiritual shepherd to his Tarascan people, so he entered Bible school to be prepared for the ministry. There he found a wonderful Christian wife. They had four children, all of whom became missionaries.

The task of evangelizing the Tarascan Indians was not easy. Ismail was often beaten up. Once they left him for dead on an Indian trail, but the Lord watched over him and saved him. He was chosen by God to take the message to the Tarascan people.

And it all started when he listened to that recording in his own language.

> *To listen to a recording in Ismail's language, which is called Purepecha, go to: globalrecordings.net/en/program/C37440*

Off the Beaten Track

Colin Stott

INDIA

What a night! Heavy rains had fallen, making quagmires of the narrow, soft dirt roads that linked scattered farming villages in India.

Mild mannered Mathai casually observed, "This is bad driving tonight," as he carefully maneuvered their jeep through the mud and inky blackness of the night in rural India.

No sooner had Mathai made his observation than the wheels hit an extremely slippery section of the narrow road. Someone shouted, "We're sliding over the side!" The men jumped from the jeep, slipping and stumbling in the mud. They pushed and grunted, called for advice, and offered quickly breathed prayers. Finally their efforts proved successful and the vehicle was back on the road.

Once more they headed in the direction of a place where they could rest their weary bodies. They would need the rest before the new day dawned. And each day would bring more of the unknown.

What had brought these five men from their homes in the city? Each had become a new creation in Christ. They wanted to share their faith with their countrymen in these isolated villages who had never heard of Jesus.

The farmers and their families work long, back-breaking hours. They till the stubborn soil without the aid of modern equipment and have little to show for their labor. In vain efforts to protect themselves from evil spirits, they faithfully bow in obeisance before Hindu gods and bring offerings of flower garlands, coconuts and garden produce to place on the temple altars.

The team had come to villagers such as these. In order to communicate the way of salvation in the local dialects, they had brought a supply of GRN players and recordings.

They approached the first village, not knowing what to expect. Would the people be willing to pay—even a small sum of money—for a player from their meager earnings? Would they accept the free recordings? Would they listen? Would they drive them off?

Stares greeted them as they entered. Who are these strangers? What is their business here? One team member began to play a recording. Villagers put water jugs and baskets down. They stood still and faced in the direction of the sound. Instead of hostility there were smiles and curiosity. Soon a few hands were delving into small purses or untying the knots in loincloths. Money was extracted and quickly exchanged for the simple players. Eager hands reached out to receive the recordings.

The team continued until 35 villages had been visited and the stock of players and recordings was exhausted. Keen interest soon replaced cautious curiosity in every village, making it clear that the Lord had prepared the way.

In one village a Hindu priest listened and waved his arms. "Let me have your recordings." He quickly disappeared into the temple with them. Suddenly the sounds of a Christian message came booming over the temple's loudspeaker. The priest explained, "The entire village must hear these recordings. I will play them every day to make sure they do hear!"

The five men had given a few more of India's millions a chance to hear. They had to make their way home and leave the results in God's hands, confident in His promise that "faith comes by hearing."

Kathmandu Connection

Clair Rulison

NEPAL - The Sonaaha language

Embers crackled in the little fire pit. The soft, steady breathing of his parents and the children lying on mats beside him made Sagunu feel drowsy. He pulled the tattered blanket closer, trying not to disturb his wife, and stared up at the hut's woven ceiling. He heard the constant rumbling of the river as it flowed on and on, never changing much from day to day, year after year. Again tomorrow Sagunu would spend the day fishing, and maybe panning for gold as his people, the Sonaaha, had done for generations on the banks of the Kamali River in west Nepal.

This night he dwelt on the time, many years ago, when two foreigners and a Nepali interrupted his mundane life.

They taught him amazing stories, and then asked him to repeat them to a strange looking machine. He would never forget the sound of his voice coming back to him, how his friends standing around all smiled and jumped and how those words later changed his life. The God of those stories was so different, so kind, and so close. Now he knew that God was right there with him, with his family. Sagunu heard the groan of his wife and turned toward her. She seemed to be getting worse...

The short beep from his watch reminded Mr. K. that he would have to leave his office to make his appointment at 5:00 p.m. Driving through the streets of Stuttgart, he thought about the reply received from his email to GRN. For years he had taken an interest in GRN's work among people who are completely unreached by the Gospel, periodically making substantial contributions toward projects to reach them. Lately he had been drawn to efforts being made in Nepal. He imagined life in a remote Nepali village as he thought about the names of the unreached tribes that GRN had sent him. He decided to choose three from among them.

"It's 7 a.m. in Greenville, and here is the latest news..." Jean switched off the alarm clock and prepared for her time of prayer before getting caught up in the events of the day. The work of GRN in Nepal sat at the top of her prayer list. She'd supported the mission in prayer for years, and knew that despite what had already been accomplished in Nepal much had yet to be done. Lord, please advance your kingdom among the many in Nepal who have never heard your Good News.

"Praise God, this is a big step! Listen to this." The young man in Kathmandu waved an envelope and his co-worker stopped to listen. "Mr. K. has decided to contribute toward bringing the Gospel to the Hayu, the Thami and the Sonaaha. We will be able to buy players, make copies of our recordings, and visit their villages." As staff of GRN, they were very grateful for this gift – not only for what it would buy, but also for the focus it would bring to their work, where so many unreached groups pulled at their hearts. They bowed in prayer.
"Dear Father, thank you for providing for these people who so need to know you. Make them willing to receive us. Lead us to language helpers, so we can record messages. And, Lord, we need other Nepali Christians to help us distribute the tapes and disciple new believers. Thank you, Father, we're expecting answers!"

It was a relief to finally arrive at the clinic. Sagunu had done what he could in the village; let his wife rest, made many offerings on her behalf – nothing worked. There was no choice but to make the three-hour journey with Champa, which might make her worse. As he and his wife waited for the doctor, three Nepali men walked in, talking together.
One of them caught his eye. Sagunu was certain that he had

seen him before. Listening to their conversation, his eyes grew
wide. They spoke of recording messages in the Sonaaha
language. Recording! The man he recognized was one of the
three who had come to his village to make those records.

He jumped up, fumbled toward them and offered excited
respect. He did not want to let go of their hands. For the next few
hours, Sagunu asked the men many questions about the God in
their stories. Their answers were like healing medicine to an
aching heart. He knew that they spoke the truth, that he needed
God.

He wanted to follow this Jesus Christ. But would his neighbors
understand his decision? Would they reject him, not eat with
him, not invite him to village celebrations?

The men prayed hard for him that he would remain firm. They
said they would try to come to his village before long, to tell
others the same good news.

Eight people stood on the dusty road, waiting for the bus that
would take them back to Kathmandu. Until moments earlier,
they had talked excitedly together, sometimes singing. Now a
peaceful weariness had settled on them, and each silently
reflected on the past few victorious days. Twenty-three Sonaaha
had asked Jesus to be the Savior and Lord of their lives.

When the news got around, there would be rejoicing among
those who had given, prayed, and worked to bring the Good
News to the Sonaaha.

Jean turned off the lamp and lay down on her bed. Father, it is
wonderful to hear of the victory you've won among the Sonaaha.
Yet the battle has just begun, hasn't it? Protect them, Lord, and
guide them into greater and greater knowledge of Yourself.
Please help us to continue to pray for them. And, Lord there are
also the Hayu and the Thami ...

You can listen to the Sonaaha language at:
globalrecordings.net/en/language/4152

In Search of a Guide

Larry DeVilbiss

MEXICO - The Pima Language

"I'm going to be gone for a week," Abelardo told his wife.

Larry DeVilbiss looked at him in amazement. It was true that Larry had just asked Abelardo to accompany him on a trip to distribute recordings among Indians, but he really hadn't expected such a ready response. Abelardo didn't know them, and had just returned the night before from a tiring two-day hike.

It wasn't until later that Larry discovered why he had cooperated so unhesitatingly and was ready to leave at a moment's notice.

Larry, Dave and Phil were on their second trip to the Mexican Pima Indians. Several weeks earlier, they had traveled down from Los Angeles to record Gospel messages in this and another language. Back in Los Angeles, they had helped to process the recordings and now were on their way back to distribute these 'talking tracts.'

Distributing the recordings and players among the Pima posed quite a problem because the tribe, while relatively small, was spread over a large area in the mountains. The men needed someone who knew the area well to guide them. They checked a number of possibilities before Abelardo's name was suggested. They prayed that they might find him and that he would be willing and available to help.

But finding him wasn't easy. A man named Ezekiel offered to guide them to the house about forty minutes' walk from the nearest road. But Abelardo was not there. They waited that day and eventually he arrived, tired after his two-and-a-half-day walk.

Part Guarojio and part Mayo, Abelardo left home at the age of nine. He later came to know the Lord, and although he had had no formal education, he had recently learned to read. He knew the Bible well, and the principles of God's Word were very evident in his life. Because he had lived in the area, he was able to guide them to the ones who were most apt to be receptive.

They would drive as far as they could, and then walk to the houses, which were often miles apart. After talking to the families, they would leave a recording and player. It was here that Abelardo again proved to be the very one they needed. Most of the other people in that area are prejudiced against the Pima, and this would have made it difficult. But their non-Pima helper, obviously chosen by God, respected them and showed the love of Christ toward them.

In conversation along the way, Larry expressed his appreciation to Abelardo for coming on the trip at such short notice and after just meeting them for the first time.

"Oh, I already knew what I had to do," he replied.

"What do you mean?" asked Larry.

"Well, before you came, I had a dream that you would be travelling this way. I knew ahead of time exactly what each of you looked like, and what you were going to do. I just waited for you to ask me!"

You can listen to the Pima language at:
globalrecordings.net/en/language/3775

His Word on my iPhone

David Derby

NEPAL, The Nepali language

My wife and I had a basic cell phone that we used to make and receive calls and do some texting. Then we heard about the 5fish.mobi app from GRN. We decided to buy a smart phone so we could learn how to share the Gospel in the various languages of people we contact. We would never have spent money on a phone, but we did because we saw the opportunity to share Christ with immigrants we meet in the USA.

We were at a party where some friends had brought a lady who recently arrived from Nepal. Our friends were trying to tell her about Jesus in English but she only partially understood.

I decided to try 5fish.mobi and, praise the Lord, I was able to find and download a message in her heart language in about a minute, with only two bars on the cell phone service. She was able to hear a Word of Life message in Nepali. She wouldn't give me my phone back until she heard the entire message. I showed our friends how to access 5fish.mobi when they got home so they could play the other Nepali messages.

We praise God and congratulate GRN for the 5fish.mobi so anyone with a smart phone can easily find and play any one of over 5,400 languages on their cell phone.

You can listen to the Nepali language at:
globalrecordings.net/en/language/6428

New Technology, Same Message

Allan Starling

Jesús 'Chucho' Loyo, Director of Buenas Nuevas (GRN Mexico) was in Culiacan, northern Mexico, for the annual outreach to migrant laborers. The camps were filled with thousands of workers, drawn to the fertile fields of Culiacan from various parts of Mexico. Between them, they spoke over a third of the country's 300 indigenous languages.

A typical family would be housed in a 10 foot square room with no electricity or running water. Their chairs were the overturned buckets used for picking tomatoes or bell peppers. Aside from a mattress on the dirt floor, their one luxury would be a cassette or CD player. The only available recordings would be in Spanish, their second language.

When teams went to native villages in southern Mexico they often received a hostile reception. But in the migrant camps the people were cordial, curious, and eager to receive a recording of the Gospel message in their heart language.

Chucho and his team arrived at a camp and went systematically door-to-door offering free recordings. The first challenge was to discover the appropriate dialect. A typical response might be, "I speak Zapotec." The interviewer had to find out which of the over 50 dialects of Zapotec the man spoke. This was accomplished by playing short segments of different dialects—a time consuming procedure. But Chucho now had a GRN app on his smartphone called 5fish and he was able to quickly play the samples. It was easy to see which sample was in the man's dialect, because his eyes would widen and he would cover his mouth to hide his smile. That led to the next challenge—making a copy of the messages for the man and his family. In former years, practically all the migrant laborers owned portable stereos, so cassettes or CDs had to be duplicated for them. Amazingly, most of these poor migrant laborers now had cell phones, even smart phones. Because the GRN recordings had been digitally re-mastered, Chucho and his team were able to reproduce them in whatever media was needed.

At another door, they met a young man who spoke a language called Mixtec Coicoyán. This young man was using his cell phone to listen to music. The words to the songs were all in Spanish. When Chucho offered him recordings in his native language, he was happy to take them. It was a simple matter to transfer them, using Bluetooth technology.

Later they met Martin, a drug-addicted Nahuatl Indian. He told them he had already received a GRN CD at the place where he collected his pay, then related the rest of his story.

"That day I was depressed and sad. I had many problems because drugs were destroying me and my family. I planned to kill myself after picking up my salary. But when I got back to my room, I had the CD in my hand so I listened to it. It was in my language and spoke to my heart. I listened right to the end. When it was over I said to God, 'If you are real, please help me. Please give me another chance.' I suddenly felt very tired and fell asleep. In my sleep I saw a bright light. A voice told me, 'You will have more time with your family.' When I woke, I realized that God had spoken to me. I knew he was real."

Chucho and the team had to move on to another camp. As they walked to their vehicles, they heard the GRN messages in different languages being played all over the camp. They knew that when the harvest was over that year, the migrant laborers would return home. They would carry with them more than 6,000 GRN recordings in 130 languages. The story of salvation by God's grace had not changed, but the new technology made it easier to spread that message to isolated villages in Oaxaca, Guerrero and other states in southern Mexico.

LISTENING TO RECORDINGS

Since Joy made those first phonograph records on the last day of 1938, the Mission has been challenged to keep up with the latest technology. To meet the needs of people living in needy situations, GRN has not only used the latest commercial machines but its engineers and technicians have devised unique players for use in areas where no electricity is available and batteries are a luxury.

Over the years, these machines have proclaimed the Good News from phonograph records, audio cassettes, and MP3's. No matter the method, the results have been the same. Thousands have heard the message and made decisions to follow Christ. The stories speak for themselves.

The Wakindiga Listen

Sanna Barlow - Light is Sown

This is a continuation of Recording the Wakindiga

TANZANIA, EAST AFRICA - The Wakindiga Language

After two and a half days making recordings, with the help of missionary Bob Ward, we returned the three Wakindiga pygmies from the mission station to their Yaida Swamps in the heart of the Tanzania, East Africa.

Long before we approached the camp, we heard the joy-cry of the Wakindigas, their treble-scale trilling, as they received the Mzee, their chief, and two men who accompanied him to Isanzu.

We were only halfway up the hillside when the people clambered down over the rocks to greet us with their happy Swahili greetings, "Jambo, Mama. Jambo, Bwana." We took part in their triple handclasp, kept our balance on the rocks, and proceeded slowly upward as our welcomers poured down upon us. They crowded around us—young people and children; women with babies slung around their backs; youths with bright beads, leather wrist charms and headbands of woven grass. After their initial greetings, we saw only smiles since their Swahili was as scant as ours; and their own language with its variety of clicks seemed to us a very part of the forest itself.

We sat under one of the two giant baobab trees that flanked their small hilltop encampment. Our hosts had neatly arranged our chairs, flat rocks, and now huddled together under the farther baobab. A soft twittering conversation blended with the night sounds of the bush around us. Nearby four or five little fires glowed red between stones.

Pastor Paulus set the recorder gently on a low stone table. Now the box was ready with eight precious messages, which it had been 'taught' to speak in the clicks and clucks of these forest pygmies. They had never before heard one whisper about that Savior whose seeking love could not pass them by.

This was a sacred hour.

The voice from the machine spoke clearly. It was not a Wazungu—a European. It was a real Wakindiga. To all but the Mzee himself, it was obvious that this was his own voice. Therefore, it spoke with the authority of the old chief to his own people.

"My Wakindiga people, for many years our fathers have not known the true God. They worshiped false gods and evil spirits. No one told them the truth about these things. But now we have the light. Listen to the Good News of the true God who loves us."

From the audience came soft low clicks of surprise and joy, then utter silence as the voice continued:

"Hear these words about His Son, Jesus Christ. He lived on this earth as a Man, and died to take away our sins. But He arose again from the dead and is living now in Heaven. He will forgive the sins of all who believe in Him.

"My people, will you also follow the light? Do you want eternal life from God? Put your trust in Jesus Christ. Ask Him to forgive your sins. Obey His words. When this life is over, it is Jesus who will take you to Heaven."

The speaker held them in utter silence, transfixed. Even the eerie wails of hyenas did not distract attention from this big voice booming out of the little box. It continued:

There is only one true God. It is He who created us. He loves us. He gave us salvation through His Son. He wants us to follow Him and worship Him only. He gives forgiveness and peace to those who believe in Jesus. He fills our hearts with joy. He cares for us as a Father cares for His children.

He has given us the Bible. It is His message to all people that they may know how to love Him and to live good lives. God has sent people to teach us how to pray that we may know how to talk to Him. His Holy Spirit is given to live in our hearts to comfort and guide us.

How can we thank God for all these good things? We can give our lives to Him, and we can refuse the dark ways of the past.

God is calling everyone - fathers, mothers, children, elders, rich and poor. Let us all give Him our hearts. Let us, by His power, live clean, good lives. Let us serve Him. Let us praise Him for Jesus Christ and His many gifts to us.

No one spoke to break the hush compelled by the marvel of these words. It was a perfect overture, touching briefly all the themes developed with closer detail in each of the other seven messages.

With only a short pause, the next message began—a dialogue with two Wakindiga greeting one another, a young lad and an old man. The youth's voice spoke out a salutation:

"You have come."

The Mzee's voice responded:

"Yes, I have come."

But at that very instant, and with electrified spontaneity, our audience also responded with the same clucking and syllable stress the old man had so carefully taught the box to imitate. Proceeding with the formal greeting, the box asked:

"And what is the news?"

Suddenly, again the semicircle in chorus answered, "The news is only good."

With a wave of his hand, the Mzee silenced his people while the two voices in the box conversed about the many who came to trade at the market; men and women from different tribes were there—Wanyiramba, Wasanzu, Wagogo, Wakindiga—along with Arabs, Indians, and Europeans as well. Then presently a riddle was introduced.

"There is One who knows the hearts of all people. His eyes see all their ways. He knows all their thoughts."

"Truly? Who is this?"

"He is God. When a man steals something and hides it in his clothes, he thinks, No one sees me. But God sees. No man can deceive God."

The conversation built up into an analysis of man's heart, and of God's complete knowledge of it; His righteous need to punish sin. At this point, the youth in the box exclaimed:

"Oh, I am grieved. I am afraid. God knows my heart also."

Then came the reply that all people are the same in this respect—the Wanyiramba, Wasanzu, Wagogo, Wakindiga, the Arab, Indian, and European. The hearts of all people are alike. All have sinful hearts.

This led naturally to a brief description of the way of escape through the Savior who bore the punishment for our sins, and of how He is able to change a person's heart. It closed with:

"Is it true? Jesus Christ can save me?"

"Yes, He alone can save you."

"Safi kabisa"—Absolutely clear, whispered the old chief repeatedly, interpreting to us the polite crescendo of Wakindiga clicks rising up out of the silence that marked the close of this second message.

"More?" we queried.

"Ndio. Asante sana"—Yes, thank you very much, came the eager reply. And so the teaching followed line upon line.

Their faces reflected intense concentration, and unspeakable wonderment. They listened to three more messages: "The Resurrection" followed by "Words about Heaven" and the last to be played that night, "Tell Me," with its closing paragraphs reiterating the name of Jesus Christ – Yesu Kristu – so they could learn to say it easily. Mzee had practiced many times in order to pronounce this name consistently.

"Nataka tena?"—Want it again?

"Ndio, ndio." The Mzee's Swahili again interpreted the low clucking applause of the eager listeners. So the box repeated the last message, closing with:

"Where is Jesus now?"

"He is now in Heaven. Yet He is very close to us. He hears our prayers."

"Will He hear me?"

"Yes, He hears all who call upon His name. Believe in Him. He will save you."

"These are good words. Thank you for telling me these good words."

"Mzuri, mzuri," whispered the Mzee, bowing in gratitude. And then again, "Sawa sawa, sawa sawa"—It is right, it is right. Over and over he said it, nodding his head. "Sawa sawa. Sawa sawa." No one else spoke.

We thought of the pygmies around us who were having their first introduction, in their own language, to One in their midst who could not forget the least of His creatures. And now His words, unencumbered by an alien voice or accent, were planting themselves like seeds of light in the hearts of all who heard. This message was overtaking the little people of the wilds, who knew well how to talk to the animals, who could smell the approach of an elephant or rhino and tell you which it is and how big. And now, what were these people thinking?

By this time it was late, and we had to return to the jeep two miles away. Near the edge of the hilltop stood the Mzee, his wrinkled face a study, his hand stretched out for the triple handshake and good-byes to each of us. The last was Bwana Bob with his gun over his shoulder. But the Wakindiga chief would not let him go without a continuous handshake. It went on and on, speaking more gratitude than could be interpreted in words. At least 22 times the Mzee clasped the Bwana's hand. At last, as we pulled ourselves away from these dear friends, the Mzee said to Bwana Bob, "Mungu na saidia."—God is helping you.

As we started down the rocky hillside toward the plain and river bottom, two young Wakindiga with bows and arrows took embers from the stone fireplaces and preceded us. They marked our way by dropping sparks of light along the path to reveal a jutting rock or a thorny branch stretching over the trail.

"This experience has been the greatest thing that has happened to me since my coming to Africa," Bob Ward said. As he spoke, we thought of his keen desire to reach the Wakindiga; and of his parting with the old chief, Mzee. By the grace of God this missionary and others like him will not stop short of planting these recordings in Wakindiga encampments. There the small boxes, which can travel with the people wherever they go, can also keep the records talking, and the seeds of light falling in abundance upon the soil from which a harvest must be intended.

You can listen to the Wakindiga language at:
globalrecordings.net/en/program/C02291

Milestones
Listening to the Messages

Allan Starling

CardTalk

When Joy Ridderhof was inspired to make recordings of the Gospel in Spanish, it was fueled by the memory of spring-wound phonographs blaring out songs in English and Spanish in the little Honduran villages where she had formerly ministered. Why not use those very machines to sound out the Christian messages and songs?

Joy thought of the words of the Apostle Paul: "How shall they hear [the Gospel] without a preacher?" She paraphrased them as, "How shall they hear [the recordings] without a player?" There were many other isolated tribes with no means of playing the recordings. So the challenge was to design and build a simple, rugged player that did not rely on electricity or batteries. With God's help, this was accomplished.

The introduction of the Phonette heralded the first big milestone in the supply of players to primitive peoples. Countless of these players, powered by 'elbow grease' and encased in either wood, metal or plastic, were sent around the world to play 78 rpm records in hundreds and later thousands of languages. The CardTalk – an expendable record player made almost entirely of cardboard – followed the Phonette. It was small, light and inexpensive and found its way to many inaccessible places worldwide. It could play speech, but because it was turned by hand, it could not reproduce music well without a lot of pitch fluctuations.

When phonograph records gave way to audiocassettes, the continued lack of electricity and batteries in unreached areas precluded the use of regular commercial cassette players. But someone asked: "Can't we put a small generator into a cassette player?" So a new major breakthrough came with the design and manufacture of the hand-cranked TapeTalk and Messenger players. They play any standard audiocassette with clarity. More important is the ability to turn up the volume so a crowd can gather around and hear the message in their heart language.

When CDs began replacing audiocassettes, GRN prepared itself for its biggest milestone, the switch from analog to digital. This process involved the mammoth task of digitally remastering all of their open reel tapes in thousands of languages and building a multi-terabyte server to store the digital files. It opened up enormous possibilities for making the messages available to more people in multiple ways.

People who speak any of the thousands of languages and dialects could now listen to the messages on the GRN website or follow links to other sites with evangelistic recordings. Those with high-speed Internet service, even in closed counties, could download Gospel messages for playing on Cassettes, CDs, MP3s, and cell phones or whatever new digital player comes along.

As technology advances, GRN must constantly keep in mind those who have been bypassed by the latest developments. Imagine a missionary or national Christian downloading the messages to take to the lost in their locations. Picture the hand-cranked cassette players still on duty worldwide in villages without electricity. Lastly, picture a group of unreached people in a distant location listening to the Words of Life messages coming loudly and clearly from GRN's latest Saber hand-cranked MP3 player. We could label that 'New container, Same Life-Changing Message.'

Marching to a Different Drum

Colin Stott

LIBERIA, WEST AFRICA

The old Muslim man never imagined his life would be turned upside down. For over 65 years he had been beating the drum for the men's secret society in his village, until civil war came. Great turmoil and suffering spread across his West African country of Liberia. His family fled the village. Though thankful for the refuge offered at the camps for displaced people, he missed his home.

Not only did the war uproot him, but something else happened to shake his belief system to the core. Like the rest of the townspeople, he had grown up with a strong belief in Islam. This was the only way. He remembered how some Christians had once tried to enter the village but had been forced to leave. Their different beliefs had influenced some of the villagers. Several wives, children and other family members accepted Christianity, and as a result were put out of the village.

A group of Christians visited the camp where the old man sat. They showed real concern for the people. They played recordings in the languages spoken in the camp and showed films that explained how much Jesus loves us. The message that Jesus is the only way to God rang true, and after listening closely, the old man laid aside the beliefs of a lifetime to follow Jesus Christ. No longer would he beat the drum for the men's secret society.

But who were these Christians that shared the Gospel, and how was the old man able to hear in his own language? That's a separate story.

When civil war broke out in Liberia, West Africa, nearly one in ten of the citizens were murdered and almost half of those who survived fled their homes. National GRN workers were forced to leave the country.

Later, the situation began to stabilize but it was still unsafe for many from the villages to return to their homes. They stayed in the camps. This gave many opportunities for Christians to share the Gospel with Muslims who previously would have chased them out of their villages

The GRN team, working with SIM International missionaries and a local evangelical church, formed an evangelism team to share Christ in several of the camps. They showed the Jesus film, a dramatization of Luke's Gospel, many times. In addition, they placed hundreds of evangelism recordings in many languages into the hands of the refugees and boldly preached the Gospel. There was a great openness to the Word and several thousand refugees turned to Christ. Among them were several hundred Muslims, the old man included.

He now marched to a different drum!

Timeless Messages

Allan Starling

PAPUA NEW GUINEA - The Wantoat Language

Ever since the disaster at the Tower of
Babel, the number of languages in the
world has been steadily growing.
Experts have identified some 7,000
in today's world, together with a
possible 5,000 additional dialects.
But not only has the total increased,
but individual languages are in a
constant state of change. Over a period
of 250 years, the Dutch language spoken
in South Africa changed enough to be
recognized as a language in its own right—Afrikaans. The English
language is molded not only by geography, but by history. As
much as others may admire the language of the King James
Bible, they would ridicule us if we spoke that way in our everyday
conversation.

This dynamic language growth presents problems to an
organization like GRN. It brings into question the usefulness of
audio recordings made in the earlier years of their 75 year
history. The remarkable story of Don Richter and his recordings
throws some light on the question.

In 1950 Don left the USA for Oceania with the express intention
of making audio recordings of the Gospel message for peoples in
countries like Papua New Guinea, Solomon Islands, Indonesia
and Vanuatu. Initially the equipment was primitive and the
conditions for making recordings were always far from ideal. But
Don persevered, and over the next 19 years he recorded
hundreds of languages. But with all the changes going on in that
part of the world and the encroachment of civilization, how long
would these recordings be effective?

Forty years later, that question was asked by a missionary to speakers of the Wantoat language in the Morobe Province of Papua New Guinea.

"Would they still be useful?" he wondered. "I didn't know," he told us. "But there was only one way to find out. I made 12 copies of the 'Words of Life' cassette made from Don's forty year old recordings and took them with me."

Slowly the church filled with people from around the district and he began to play the tape in their language.

As they listened to the recordings, these people who had lost interest in their New Testament found that their hearts were moved. Four speakers had been used to make the recordings. Three of them had long since died and the fourth was now very old. But these messages from beyond the grave spoke to their hearts and reawakened their thirst for God.

The people promised that it would not be long before all 8,000 speakers of that language would hear these "Words of Life" in their own language.

Another missionary to the people who speak Gapapaiwa is thrilled to play the old recordings to the people on GRN's high-tech hand-cranked Saber MP3 player. The old recordings done by Don Richter are very special to the people. They realize their fathers and grandfathers responded to the Gospel through the first recordings, but the present generation has not followed the Christian way of their forefathers and has lived in spiritual darkness. When an old man was feeling sick and ready to die, Francis played him the old recordings including a message he had spoken. God spoke to him and now he wants to live.

Lord of the Cassette Player

Dave Carson

SENEGAL, WEST AFRICA - The Wolof Language

During the six months that my wife Pam and I lived in the coastal town of Saint-Louis in the Senegal River Valley in West Africa, the study of the Wolof Language took most of my time. During that period the Lord enabled me to cultivate some good friendships and gave me many occasions to witness about Christ.

One family to whom I had become particularly close is the Wade (pronounced Wad) family, who live in the village of Pumuxor (pronounced Pumuhor) on the outskirts of Saint-Louis. The extended family lived in two neighboring compounds. Four older men had a total of 10 wives. These have several sons in their mid and late 20s and more younger children than I have ever managed to count.

Over several months of visiting the Wade family on a regular basis, I had numerous opportunities to share the Word of God with them. They were strongly Islamic. One of the men had even made the pilgrimage to Mecca. Despite this, I noticed that they always seem interested in hearing what I had to say. Admittedly, though, they showed no signs of accepting my words as the truth. I read them the Scriptures in Wolof or simply told them what Jesus did for them on the cross. One day I even told them the whole Easter story with a set of pictures. Everyone listened attentively.

One day something happened that let me know the Lord does not send us out alone to be His witnesses. He is with us every step of the way.

In my regular visits to the Wade family, I took along a player and a GRN cassette in the Wolof language. This cassette contained 10 messages. Each about three minutes long, they explained the Gospel of the Lord Jesus Christ in an interesting way.

One of the messages told of Abraham going up to sacrifice Isaac. This story is known to all Muslims, though they substitute Ishmael for Isaac. The Gospel message made the application that Jesus Christ is the Lamb of God, and He replaced us on Calvary just as the ram replaced Isaac.

I arrived at Pumuxor on a hot day and found the men and children sitting outside in the shade of the house. After greeting everyone, I showed one of the young men, Ablaay, the cassette player. He was interested and wanted to listen. The words of life came from the player, and others gathered around. The women quieted down and listened too.

After we listened to three or four messages, Ablaay jumped up and ran into the house. In a moment he came back with two cassettes. I sighed inwardly. I knew they were cassettes of Muslim preaching. Ablaay removed the tape of the Gospel and put in one of his tapes.

I wondered what to do. Should I refuse to let him use my cassette player for such devilish propaganda? Finally, I felt that I should not do anything. No sound came out of Ablaay's cassette so he tried the other. Still nothing. He reinserted the GRN cassette. Out came the Gospel message loud and clear! I thanked God for keeping the message of error from being heard.

But this wasn't the end of it.

Once again Ablaay removed the cassette of the Gospel and inserted one of his. Much to my dismay, out came the traditional Wolof music that accompanies Muslim sermons. I breathed a prayer: "Lord, don't let that tape be played in your cassette player." In a couple of seconds the player stopped. Ablaay opened it up to discover that it had 'eaten' his tape. The tape was wound up in the mechanism of the player.

"This player belongs to God and only plays cassettes about Jesus," I told Ablaay.

"But my tapes are about God," he replied.

"Yes," I said, "but is it the truth about God? This player only plays the truth." I knew that I had taken a big step of faith in saying what I did and must trust the Lord for the outcome. Ablaay managed to rewind the damaged cassette. Then he put in the other one. All that came out was an inaudible mumble with a lot of static. Finally Ablaay gave up trying to play his tapes. We all listened to the rest of the recordings tape—all 10 messages. We even repeated several of them.

What impression was formed on the minds of the ones who listened that day? I can't say for sure, but I do know that on this day the devil did not get a hearing. God is faithful. He is Lord even of the cassette player. Hallelujah.

You can listen to the Wolof language at:
globalrecordings.net/en/language/4592

"The Box Talks!"

Global Prayer Digest

SENEGAL, WEST AFRICA - The Balanta Language

"The box talks! Come and listen, come and hear! It speaks our words, Balanta!" Turning slowly from their daily activity of cultivating groundnuts, first the children and then their parents curiously approached the young man and his box that was talking. And yes, it was not the foreigner's language. It was Balanta! For the first time, the villagers were hearing about Jesus in their own language.

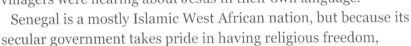

Senegal is a mostly Islamic West African nation, but because its secular government takes pride in having religious freedom, Senegal is wide open to the Gospel.

A New Tribes Missions missionary working with the Balanta, a remote group on Senegal's southern border, reports the thrill he experienced after many years of hard work. He had to leave the field for health reasons, but not before he had been able to record the Gospel and Bible lessons in the village's own language.

There may be as many as 15 believers in the village now. The Balanta are only one of 37 language groups in Senegal, many of which are oral communicators.

Gospel recordings are available in 29 of these languages. These can spearhead the 'audio cassette church,' where all the teaching is from a cassette. In the absence of a live pastor, this electronic means is a way to multiply the work of a missionary or pastor, enabling him to speak at dozens of locations via recordings. Then local workers can follow up with Bible teaching and discipleship.

You can listen to the Balanta language at:
globalrecordings.net/en/program/C01550

Double Miracle

Rob Harris

SUDAN, NORTH AFRICA - The Mabaan Language

I was staying with a missionary way out on the eastern border of Sudan. I had been struggling for two weeks with the intricacies and frustrations of recording Gospel messages in the Mabaan language. Late one evening I accompanied the doctor with whom I was staying to the dark unlit wards of Mabaan's only hospital. I held the flashlight as the doctor examined the bloated stomach of old Jumbano, a Mabaan patient in great pain from an internal obstruction. The doctor shook his head uneasily, wondering aloud if he should operate. Normally there would be no hesitation, but the hospital's operating room had been out of use for years. There was no sterile equipment. It would be almost as risky to operate as not.

After consultation with the nurses, the doctor felt that an operation would be necessary. Without it Jumbano would die. God had other plans though, because when we brought Jumbano's problem before the Lord in prayer, his answer was immediate. The obstruction was cleared naturally, or should I say supernaturally. We all praised God for this miracle.

The next day we rejoiced even more over a greater miracle. We had invited Jumbano over to the doctor's house so that he could listen to the Mabaan recordings I had recently struggled to make. He came willingly and sat under a tree, quietly listening to the wonderful news of salvation through Christ. The old man drank in the messages, often repeating phrases and acknowledging the truth of God's Word while swaying back and forth. He had once rejected Christianity, but now God's Spirit was at work in his life in convicting power.

The recording finished playing. Unable to express his feelings in our language Jumbano demonstrated them with vivid gestures. He then put his hands over his eyes trying to show us that something deep had taken place in his life. We couldn't communicate enough to know if a definite decision had been made, so we contacted the local Mabaan pastor who informed us that Jumbano had indeed given his life to Jesus while he listened.

During the following days Jumbano came back many times to listen to more of the recorded messages. He soaked up the teachings, repeating, acknowledging and hungrily taking in the truth of God's word. This gave me a new realization of God's power by His Spirit to transform lives, even through the simple means of a recorded message.

You can listen to the Mabaan language at: globalrecordings.net/en/program/C12040

Ashtar Finds Peace

Eddie and Daphne Smith

CHAD, CENTRAL AFRICA - The Massalit Language

Ashtar felt ill. The swelling under her arm made it more and more difficult for her to grind her millet. She did not realize that she was dying of cancer.

Ashtar was from a large tribe called the Massalit in Chad. She never went to school and understood that being born a girl in a Muslim country, she was worth only one third the value of a man. She had worked since she was five, was married before she was 14, and was now a widow. Her only son was in his teens. If her husband were alive he would have reminded her that the prophet said, 'Hell was created for women!' What hope had she of paradise?

There was no medicine at the hospital and all we could give her was aspirin. As her health declined, we brought her food and a player with recordings in the local Arabic dialect.

As she listened to the recorded message, something touched her heart. It taught her of a Prophet who had come to tell her that God loved her. He had angered the self-righteous religious people and He cared for women! She lay back and listened without really understanding. But as she played the messages over and over again she started to grasp what was being said. Light came into her heart. She heard words that in the midst of her pain spoke peace to her.

She amazed her son when he visited. He saw a dying woman but she had no fear. His mother radiated peace.

We were away at a conference when Ashtar died. When we returned we heard that she had refused to say the customary

Muslim declaration on her deathbed. She had declared instead that she believed in Jesus the Christ.

As a consequence, her mouth was stuffed with dirt and her body was buried in an unmarked grave, in a location not even known to her son. However, there is a Massalit woman in heaven with the Lord, because of God's grace and two missionaries with a cassette that gave her the good news of salvation in Christ.

Women of many other tribes in Chad are brought up to toil and suffer. They have been physically abused at initiation, have borne children, been widowed or cast off, not knowing that there is a God who loves them. Will they hear of God's love through the recordings?

You can listen to the Massalit language at:
globalrecordings.net/en/language/3512

Voices from the Past

Larry Allmon

NIGERIA, WEST AFRICA - The Tangale Language

In 1962, our veteran recordist, Ann Sherwood, painstakingly made recordings for the Tangale people of Nigeria. She described the Tangales as being pagan, semi-primitive, and semi-literate.

In order to evaluate the effectiveness of our recordings, we enclose a simple questionnaire in each parcel. Twenty eight years after the original recordings, we received such a 'report card' from a SIM missionary in Nigeria. She reported that the Tangale recordings had been taken to a number of their villages and that "six persons had been saved for sure, and 50 more were asking for special prayers for repentance."

This young missionary could hardly stop with just the statistics, so she penned this memo on the back of the card.

"Two of the voices on the Tangale tape are the voices of a young man's father and grandfather. Both are dead now and the son, Gowan, had strayed far from the Christian home in which he was brought up. When he listened to the tape, he heard his father and grandfather asking him to repent! As a result, he gave his life to Christ. His common law wife also accepted Jesus.

"Then they shared with their neighbor, Dowdo, and his common law wife, and they too both repented and accepted Christ. All four stood up in church and gave public testimony of repentance and confession of sin. They are all in a baptism class now, and looking forward to taking wedding vows to be legally married. Praise be to Jesus for your recordings!"

As far back as 1962, God had been preparing to speak to Gowan and his friends about their future repentance in 1990.

You can listen to the Tangale language at: globalrecordings.net/en/program/C00591

An Evening in the Andes

Sara Corson

PERU - The Aymara Language

The twilight deepened and it was getting difficult to see faces clearly. Banana trees waved in the evening breeze, their broad leaves outlined against a sky studded with the stars of the Southern Hemisphere. Around us the peaks of the Andes Mountains pointed into the sky. In this secluded place I sat with my Indian brothers and sisters. We shivered in the cool breeze of the evening.

The local Aymara church leader, Caludio, and I had climbed the steep path in the twilight to the yard of one of the believers. A group of 25 Aymara Indians sat in a circle, the women sitting together on flour sacks.

A little out of breath, Claudio greeted the others and took his place among the men. "The last time we met," Claudio began, "We had visitors from the United States who came to bring us greetings and to share a message with us. They gave us this player with tapes in our language."

The men crowded around as Claudio took a cassette player out of a sack and showed them how it worked without the need of electricity or batteries.

"We just turn this crank and it talks," he said.

Everyone was tired after a long day's work, and watched as Claudio put the cassette in the player and began to turn the crank. The player's gears and generator made a soft purring sound.

Suddenly beautiful and clear voices rang out singing a song in the Aymara language. An older woman who had just arrived sat

114

immobile for a minute wearing a puzzled look. She was obviously trying to figure out where these lovely voices were coming from. Since the singing came from Claudio's direction, she jumped up to peer over his shoulder. She laughed with delight when she saw the player being cranked. It was speaking and singing her language!

The preachers and church workers who occasionally visit these remote Indians of the Andes are normally Spanish speaking. Most of the Aymara men and some of the women understand Spanish, but to have a cassette in their own language was something special. They all listened with rapt attention to the short messages and songs about Jesus and His power to save.

The segments on the cassette were intended to be used one at a time, but everyone kept asking to hear more. For an hour these Aymara Indians played the cassette, taking turns at the crank. This gave them a chance to participate and feel good at having a part in producing the sound. As the cassette came to an end for the third time, everyone shouted, "Let's hear it again!"

As a visitor and an outsider, it was a great privilege to witness the planting of seeds of faith that no doubt will produce fruit in the hearers' lives.

As I witnessed the scene, I wished that the missionaries who made these recordings and special players could spend just one evening with these people high in the Andes Mountains of South America. I wished they could see the joy on their faces as they listened to the message of Jesus and sang along with hymns of their own language.

You can listen to the Aymara language at:
globalrecording.net/en/language/7

The Flipped Peso

Ralph L. Bartholomew

MEXICO

Bill Cornthwaite closed the lid on the record press and waited for a moment for the heated plastic to fill in all the grooves. After a few seconds of cooling, he opened it and removed the newly made record.

Again he reached for another preheated plastic blob, placed it in the center of the chrome stamper, and clamped down the lid. And while he waited, he glanced over at the volunteer helping him at GRN's small factory in Puebla, Mexico. He noticed how intently Adelberto Cen, a young Mayan Indian, was listening to the record in his native language playing over the loud speaker.

Just as it ended, Adelberto looked up and laughed. "I'm going to play it again" he grinned.

"Oh, no," Bill teased. "You've played it 10 times already this afternoon."

"That's my favorite record," Adelberto told him, "That's the one that brought me to the Lord."

"I didn't know that," Bill answered. "Tell me about it."

"Sure. I was a farm laborer, as most of my people are," he began. "One day I went into town to buy food for my wife. We had been married only six months. I passed a small chapel that had a loudspeaker nailed on the door. It was playing this record about Jesus being the great high priest. I walked past it three times so I could hear the whole story.

"I was stricken in my heart and I knew God was speaking to me. But I also knew I couldn't go into that kind of a church. So I walked down to the market, but God would not leave me alone.

"I walked around a bit, but I knew I must resolve this thing some way. Suddenly I felt a silver peso in my pocket. Good, I'll flip it. If the eagle came up, I'd go back. If not, I'd forget all about it.

"I flipped. The eagle came up. So I went back, and the people at the church led me to the Lord. When I went home and told my wife, she threw up her hands, packed and went home to her family. Six months later she came back and I was able to lead her to the Lord. Now I'm preparing to be a pastor to my own people."

Bill smiled and silently thanked God for calling him into this work, and for trophies of God's grace like Adelberto.

Tell Me More

Colin Stott

TIBET, CHINA - The Kham language

"Welcome, welcome," said a Tibetan nomad. "Come, sit down and have something to eat."

Our new friend introduced us to his wife and four children. After we had eaten, I took a Gospel from my bag. I told him it was a book about Jesus and that in other parts of China there are many followers of Jesus. He wanted to know more, so I offered him a recording in the Kham Tibetan dialect.

I also took out a large flipchart of pictures, which along with the recording, explains the way of salvation from creation to the resurrection.

The family was glued to the book as I turned the pages to synchronize with the recording. Before leaving we prayed together, and our Tibetan friend invited Jesus to come and live with them in their home.

As we departed he took out the book and continued to explain the Bible stories to the family.

You can listen to the Tibetan Kham language at: globalrecordings.net/en/program/C62870

From Shiva to Christ

Colin Stott

INDIA

My name is Harish Malani. My family is Hindu and they worship a god named Shiva as their main family deity. I grew up doing all the religious rituals and took a deep interest in obeying all of them. Every day I would enter our family worship room and bow down before the deities. On special days, I would bathe the idols and change their clothes.

Although I became very successful in business, deep inside I felt dissatisfied and empty. I wanted to go to heaven, but when I checked with my Hindu priests about how I could get there, I was told my good deeds had to exceed my bad deeds. As I checked my life, I found that there was good on the outside. But inside things were not so good. I lied often, got into fights with neighbors and sometimes beat up my wife. I indulged in alcohol and gambling.

All of this made me dejected and miserable. I came to the conclusion that there cannot be a heaven because if we are all sinners, no one could enter and heaven would be an empty place. This probably meant there was no God at all.

One day while visiting a friend, he gave me a cassette in my Hindi language produced by GRN. I heard a message about the sinful heart of man and the existence of heaven and hell. God opened my understanding and showed me we can do nothing to free ourselves from sin. Jesus Christ alone can save us and forgive us. When I believed on the Lord Jesus, the burden of sin left me, and I sensed a deep peace within my heart.

From that day my life started to change. When I felt bitter, God took the bitterness away. When I could not love others, the love of God started flowing from me. I saw my addiction to alcohol and my anger disappear. I found myself in love with God and I devoured His Word.

I received a lot of opposition from family and friends. Yet, they acknowledge the powerful God at work within me. They sometimes ask me to pray for them. I trust one day they will experience the newness of life in Christ Jesus.

Deliverance from Kali

Colin Stott

INDIA

Katta Sai was an ardent worshiper of Kali, the Hindu goddess of death and wrath. Because he feared her, he often left his offerings at the temple even though his family had to go without food or money.

Frustrated with life, Katta Sai began to hate himself and joined a group of troublemakers who often disrupted church services and ridiculed Christians. One day, Katta Sai suddenly fell ill. Tests revealed he was in an advanced stage of cancer. He knew that death was tapping at his door.

About this time, a local pastor gave Katta Sai a GRN cassette in his Telugu language. The message of Jesus healing the blind man brought so much peace to him that he invited the pastor to pray for him. He regretted the trouble he had brought on the Christians in his village and began to cry uncontrollably. The pastor prayed with him and shared the love and forgiveness of Jesus.

The Lord miraculously touched Katta Sai. He received the Lord's healing in his soul and body and was baptized. Today Katta Sai and his family are believers and boldly stand for Jesus.

The Power of Storytelling

Ross Lange

Storytelling has always been an effective way to communicate. When Jesus was on earth, he often taught by means of stories and parables.

For years Global Recordings Network has followed Christ's method and used storytelling to communicate spiritual truths, often with amazing results.

Indonesia

A missionary was still learning the language, so he decided to begin to evangelize the people by using GRN recordings. The people were amazed that the little box was speaking their language. They looked it over carefully. Surely, they reasoned, it must be God speaking to them, since only God could speak their language.

After listening for a few minutes, they all jumped up and ran screaming into the jungle. They were not seen again for days. Why? The missionary had been playing the story of Noah. When the people heard God telling them about a great flood, they thought they had better get out of there quick before the flood came!

Burkina Faso, West Africa

The mission organization, WEC International, planned to send a couple to plant churches among an unevangelized tribe in the West African country of Upper Volta (now Burkina Faso). However, some problems arose and the couple never did make it to Africa. But around that time, GRN was able to visit that tribe and make recordings for them.

Years later, WEC sent another couple to that same tribe. When they arrived they were amazed to find that this so-called unevangelized tribe already knew about Jesus, and had memorized all those Bible stories from the recordings. They had known all about salvation for 15 years before any missionary arrived!

Today people are still captivated and convicted by the Bible stories on our recordings. A Muslim leader in Liberia said, "Your message has troubled my heart." Another Muslim in the same area said, "If the message would have reached me before, I would not have joined the Muslim faith."

Zimbabwe, Southern Africa

A Christian worker quotes someone who said, "If it weren't for your recordings, I wouldn't know Jesus as my Savior."

And so the old, old story, simply told, is still pointing many on a new path to the Lord.

Freedom from Darkness

Colin Stott

Names have been changed for security reasons

The desire to reach out with the Gospel here is so strong that the leaders want to open a GRN supply center. "We really need to supply these recordings and picture booklets for our pastors and evangelists to use. We are willing to make ourselves available to the ministry so it can be here."

As the eyes of the world have focused on the recent war, we have seen freedom come to a people held by the power of an evil dictator whose grip they could not escape. Another war has waged at the same time. This invisible war is for the souls of men also held in bondage by an evil ruler.

I was in a meeting with 25 pastors and church leaders. I was so encouraged by their comments over the use of GRN materials. One pastor said he was told by his people, "We have gone to church for seven years and have never understood these [truths] before."

Several pastors said the people just kept listening to the tapes. When some were told there were no tapes in their home-languages, they said, "Why are you discriminating against us? We need this message as well."

I talked to a man in charge of translation projects and quoted someone who told me, "I can show you many men in ministry today who first heard the Gospel from your tapes on a hand-crank player."

His face broke out in a broad smile and said, "I am one of them as well!"

From Cattle Thief to Shepherd

Jim Mittlestedt

MEXICO - The Haustec language

The Huasteco young man stood in his field, pondering the question common to all races, Why did God make us? Nicolas was typical of these hill people in the state of Chiapas, Mexico. He was a cattle thief, liquor maker, and had arranged for a woman to be murdered. His life was empty and without peace. His drinking was an escape.

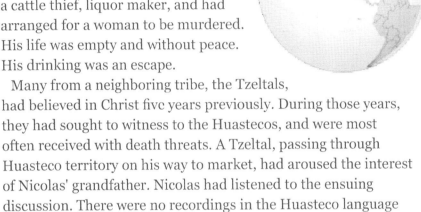

Many from a neighboring tribe, the Tzeltals, had believed in Christ five years previously. During those years, they had sought to witness to the Huastecos, and were most often received with death threats. A Tzeltal, passing through Huasteco territory on his way to market, had aroused the interest of Nicolas' grandfather. Nicolas had listened to the ensuing discussion. There were no recordings in the Huasteco language at that time but the Tzeltal man promised to send back other believers with some recordings in the related Tzotzil dialect.

Upon hearing the recordings, Nicolas thought about the message. It is good! He went back to tell his family of the words he had heard. Even at that time he began to stop drinking. But family and friends taunted him. His wife kept putting liquor in front of him. On one occasion, Nicolas cocked his arm to hit her but did not follow through. He himself took note that a change had started in him.

Nicolas retreated to the fields. There he was alone, away from the pressure of Huasteco influences. He thought about the messages he had heard from the recordings and the Tzeltals. He sought a flaw so that he could reject them. After all, if he accepted them he would be one against 8,000. To become a

Christian was to become an enemy of the tribe. But the messages were good, only good.

Today, Nicolas is the leader of a congregation of several hundred Huasteco believers. For when he received the messages, he received the Christ of the messages. From then on, he was not alone but walked with the Good Shepherd who was seeking the lost sheep of his tribe.

You can listen to the Huastec language at: globalrecordings.net/en/language/4381

THE UNFINISHED TASK

We praise God for what has been accomplished since the work began. But we are also aware that much more needs to be accomplished.

"Why didn't you come sooner?" is the question GRN field recordists have heard repeatedly.

One story tells of a language group that has heard no witness of Christ for over 400 years. Countless others wait to hear.

Who Gets the Credit?

Warren Myers - Heart and Vision

AFRICA - The Pygmies

It is hard enough to muster up concern for someone we've never met, let alone a little known tribe of African pygmies. But God put a burden on the heart of a Christian girl in New York, USA, for these people. She started praying for them and wrote to missionaries in the region, sending money to help reach the tribe.

But pygmies are nomads, constantly roaming to new forests, and the missionaries were unable to find and evangelize them. Never strong in health, the girl prayed for ten years, then died.

Another ten years passed.

One summer a man from GRN discovered the tribe. Using interpreters, he was able to record the Gospel and basic Christian truths in the tribe's language. Months later hundreds of recordings were made that brought the good news to the tribe.

The response was spectacular. As these nomadic people heard about Jesus in their language, the Holy Spirit began to work. Within a few months 80% of them had turned to God from worshipping the spirits of the trees, water, fire and the dead. Missionaries were amazed at the rapid response. Then some of them recalled the burden of the young girl who, through prayer, had prepared the ground for this advance of the Gospel.

Who gets the credit for what the Lord did in that pygmy tribe? The GRN worker, the missionaries or the girl in New York? One possible answer is summarized in I Samuel 30:24-25 NIV, "The share of the man who stayed with the supplies is to be the same as that of him who went down to the battle. All will share alike."

In another sense, none of us can take any credit, because lives can only be changed by God's mercy and grace. But we see two things here. God did it. People acted obediently and received God's recognition. They can look forward to hearing Him say one day, "Well done, my good and faithful servant (Matt. 25:21)."

No Witness in 400 Years

Colin Stott

CHINA

Recently a team came to our town for a retreat. Before going home they wanted to spend some time in a local village. We took them for the day and drove them up a windy, rough road to a village our team had yet to visit.

We were greeted at the edge of the village by a local family and were able to visit several homes. One home in particular caught our eye. It was covered in bright white plaster instead of the typical mud bricks. A man was working outside. We asked if he had built the house himself. He told us he had been building it for seven years. Now it was nearly finished.

Through an interpreter, a teammate asked him how long his family had been living in the village. He said he wasn't quite sure, but it was around 400 years. We asked if he had heard of Jesus and he said no.

For 400 years his ancestors had lived in that tiny village secluded from the rest of the world, and unaware that a Savior had died to secure their eternity.

Power to Change Lives

Colin Stott

PHILIPPINES - The Subanen language

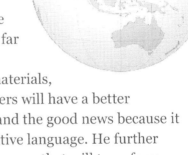

The blind old village chief chuckled. "This is one of the happiest moments in my life. I can hear the Gospel in my own language." Then he stopped and shook his head. "I wish the rest of my Subanen tribe could hear too, but there are so few missionaries to take the message to them, and we are so far away."

Now, with the arrival in of GRN materials, the chieftain believes that the villagers will have a better opportunity to receive and understand the good news because it is now delivered to them in their native language. He further believes that the Gospel will be the power that will transform their lives.

"Now, we don't have to wait for the uncertain visit of missionaries. All we do is crank the player and we can hear the Gospel without having someone to interpret. Thank God!"

While much of the island of Mindanao is evangelized, millions of people are still without a Gospel witness. Many of the cultural minorities are still in a dark spiritual condition. GRN is determined more than ever to reach these people with the good news so they can experience the same joy like the old chief.

You can listen to the Subanen language at:
globalrecordings.net/en/program/C10551

No News is Not Good News!

Colin Stott

"No news is good news" so goes the old cliché. But when it comes to preaching the Gospel, the opposite is true. God has given us some vivid reminders that sharing the Good News is urgent.

India

A man in India who was over 100 years old heard the Gospel in his language on a recording for the first time. He said to one of our coworkers, "I am an old man. Why has it taken you so long to bring this good news?"

Liberia

John Deguah, the leader of GRN in Liberia, West Africa, visited a small tribe named the Gbii to tell them about Jesus. His arrival at one of their villages coincided with the death of an old man.

The villagers were curious about what kind of news John had to bring them. After the man was buried, God gave John much boldness to clearly tell the people about Jesus.

The people were amazed at what they heard. Some wept. Many gave their lives to Christ, including the village Chief. However, the man whose father had died approached John and said, "When did this God give you this message?" John replied, "God gave this message a long time ago."

The man grasped John and shook him with all his might and in tears said, "God gave you this message and you did not come to tell us until my mother, son and father died!! I will tell this God to put their blood on your head for not coming in time to save my family."

John broke down in tears and asked the man to forgive him for not reaching his people in time. He also apologized to the people of the village. Although he arrived too late for some, praise God that through John's ministry, a church was established in the village.

As we reach out to more and more unevangelized peoples, may God enable us to not be any later than we already are.

FURTHER RESOURCES

Faith by Hearing
The Story of Gospel Recordings - Phyllis Thompson
A short, easy to read book that takes the reader from the making of the first record to reaching around the world with Gospel messages.

Count It All Joy
The Biography of Joy Ridderhof - Phyllis Thompson
This is an incredible, true story of a lady who cared for the lost, but realized that she wouldn't be able to reach the world with the Gospel message on her own. It's a very down to earth biography, outlining the struggles that many people are faced with when looking to the Lord for guidance.
Joy had an urgency regarding people who had never heard a voice telling them about Jesus Christ. The story unwinds with lots of adventure and heart-stopping moments. It is also a testimony to the love, care and provision of God and demonstrates the power of prayer.

The GRN website
Find out more about the ministry of GRN worldwide. Watch short videos at:
globalrecordings.net/en/testimonials

Subscribe to free GRN USA publications and prayer letters at
globalrecordings.net/en/subscribe/us

ACKNOWLEDGMENTS

Editing and Proofing
Colin Stott and Allan Starling collected these stories from mission publications, interviews and books now out-of-print. Sue Starling typed them into the computer. Rebecca Farnbach, Peter Lundell, Lynda Quinn, and Mary Kay Moody, all members of the San Diego Christian Writers Guild, assisted Allan in editing the stories. Dale Rickards and Irene King did the final proofreading. Most of the accounts were written by GRN staff members for the mission's publications. Others gave permission.

Authors and Contributors
Our grateful thanks goes to those who have provided the amazing stories.

Made in the USA
San Bernardino, CA
15 July 2014